Teilhard's Mass

Teilhard de Chardin, New York, 1955

"As far as my strength will allow me, because I am a priest, I would henceforth be the first to become aware of what the world loves, pursues, suffers. I would be the first to seek, to sympathize, to toil; the first in self fulfillment, the first in self denial—I would be more widely human in my sympathies and more nobly terrestrial in my ambitions than any of the world's servants....

"That is why I have taken on my vows and my priesthood (and it is this that gives me my strength and my happiness), in a determination to accept and divinize the powers of the earth....

"I speak to you, my fellow-priests, who share the battle: if there be any among you who are at a loss in so unforeseen a situation—with your mass unsaid and your ministry unaccomplished—remember that over and above the administration of the sacraments, as a higher duty than the care of individual souls, you have a universal function to fulfill: the offering to God of the *entire* world....

"You are the leaven spread by providence throughout the battlefield, so that, by your mere presence, the huge mass of our toil and agony may be transformed.

"Never have you been more priests than you are now, involved as you are and submerged in the tears and blood of a generation—never have you been more active—never more fully in the line of your vocation.

"I thank you, my God, in that you have made me a priest—and a priest ordained for War."

"The Priest"—Teilhard writing in July 1918,
awaiting word of the next engagement in World War I

Teilhard's Mass

Approaches to
"The Mass on the World"

Thomas M. King, S.J.

Paulist Press
New York/Mahwah, N.J.

Cover design by Cynthia Dunne
Book design by Lynn Else

Library of Congress Cataloging-in-Publication Data

King, Thomas Mulvihill, 1929-
    Teilhard's mass : approaches to The mass on the world / Thomas M. King.
        p. cm.
    Includes bibliographical references and index.
    ISBN 0-8091-4328-3 (alk. paper)
    1. Teilhard de Chardin, Pierre. 2. Teilhard de Chardin, Pierre. Messe sur le monde. 3. Mass. 4. Catholic Church—Liturgy. I. Teilhard de Chardin, Pierre. Messe sur le monde. English. II. Title.

    BX2230.3.K56 2005
    264'.02—dc22

                                                                    2004029063

Published by Paulist Press
997 Macarthur Boulevard
Mahwah, New Jersey, 07430

www.paulistpress.com

Printed and bound in the
United States of America

CONTENTS

ACKNOWLEDGMENTS

page ii   Frontispiece of Teilhard in New York. Photo by Philippe Halsman.

page xiv   Sketch of Teilhard. Courtesy of MIT Press, artist unidentified.

               Sketch of Emile Licent, SJ. Courtesy of MIT Press, artist unidentified.

page 5   Photo of Teilhard with his family. Courtesy of the French Teilhard de Chardin Association. Used with permission.

page 10 &   Photo of Teilhard offering Mass. Courtesy of the Mémorial
back cover   de Verdun, Musée de la Bataille. Used with permission.

page 12   Photo of Teilhard on expedition in China. Courtesy of Georgetown University archives. Used with permission.

page 18   Photo of Teilhard in India. Courtesy of Georgetown University archives. Used with permission.

page 20   Photo of the Chou-Kou-Tien team. Courtesy of Georgetown University archives. Used with permission.

page 25   Photo of Teilhard in the Western Hills of Peking. Courtesy of Georgetown University archives. Used with permission.

page 53   Map of the Ordos. Courtesy of the author. Used with permission.

page 58   Sketch of stone tools found by Teilhard and Licent. Courtesy of MIT Press, artist unidentified.

page 120   Teilhard's "holy card" of the Sacred Heart. Courtesy of Georgetown University archives. Used with permission.

page 145   Text of "The Mass on the World" taken from *The Hymn of the Universe* by Teilhard de Chardin, English translation © 1965 by William Collins, Ltd., London and Harper & Row Inc. New York.

INTRODUCTION

Ten days after my priestly ordination, I went to Quebec to study French. I soon was visiting bookstores and came across a collection of essays by Teilhard that included his twenty-page prayer/essay, *"La Messe sur le monde."* At the time I was settling into my own priesthood, and as I read and reread *"La Messe"* it began shaping my understanding of what I did daily at the altar. Later in Paris, I talked with Mlle. Jeanne Mortier (the lady who arranged for the posthumous publication of Teilhard's writings). While speaking of several of his works, she asked about my personal favorite. I replied without hesitation, *"La Messe sur le monde."* She smiled and said, *"Moi aussi."* Knowing that Teilhard often told of modifying the text, I asked if she had different versions. She said she was given only a single text: ten undated pages neatly typed with no corrections or additions.

I have come to realize I am not the only one moved by Teilhard's "Mass." In 1995 Pope John Paul II celebrated the fiftieth anniversary of his own priesthood by writing *Gift and Mystery.* There he used a text from Teilhard's "Mass" to say what the Mass meant to him: the Eucharist is "celebrated in order to offer 'on the altar of the whole earth the world's work and suffering' in the beautiful words of Teilhard de Chardin."[1] The text seems to have stayed with the Holy Father, for in his recent encyclical on the Eucharist, *Ecclesia de Eucharistia* (April 2003), he uses Teilhard's image: he told of every Mass having a "cosmic character. Yes, cosmic! Because even when it is celebrated on the humble altar of a country church, the Eucharist is always in some way celebrated on the altar of the world."[2] Cardinal Ratzinger has written a book on the liturgy in which he spoke positively of Teilhard's "Mass" and ended with a brief summary of its message:

Teilhard went on to give a new meaning to Christian worship: the transubstantiated Host is the anticipation of the transformation and divinization of matter in the christological "fullness." In his view, the Eucharist provides the movement of the cosmos with its direction; it anticipates its goal and at the same time urges it on.[3]

Though a cosmic understanding of the Mass is found in some early church writers, it was not part of recent theology until it was developed by Teilhard.

In telling of the cosmic meaning of the Mass, Teilhard spoke of the "Extensions of the Eucharist." That is, the Host of bread is "continually being encircled more closely by another, infinitely larger Host, which is nothing less than the universe itself....Thus when the phrase *'Hoc est Corpus meum'* is pronounced, *'hoc'* means *'primario'* the bread; but *'secundario,'* in a second phase occurring in nature, the matter of the sacrament is the world, throughout which there spreads, so to complete itself, the superhuman presence of the universal Christ. The world is the final, and the real, Host into which Christ gradually descends, until his time is fulfilled."[4]

Teilhard ended his "Mass on the World" "Ordos, 1923," suggesting it was written in the Ordos Desert on his first expedition in China. But he had earlier versions, most notably an essay that he called "The Priest," written in 1918 while serving in the French army in World War I. As with the later "Mass," he found himself without what he needed to offer Mass, so he offered instead a spiritual Mass: "Since today, Lord, I your Priest have neither bread nor wine nor altar, I shall spread my hands over the whole universe and take its immensity as the matter of my sacrifice."[5] He further developed these themes in writing his "Mass on the World." Though neither of the texts refers to the Mass properly speaking, each was written with a sense of his own sacramental priesthood. In writing of his "Mass" he spoke of an "extended sense" of the Eucharist. Later he would develop what could be called an "extended sense of the priesthood," for he would say each "Christian has a sacred priestly vocation";[6] he would speak of "a lay quasi priest *[un quasi pretre laic]*."[7] Additional passages make evident this wider priesthood: "In our hands, in the hands of all of us, the world and life *(our world, our life)* are placed like a Host, ready to be charged with the divine influence."[8] He came to see all of us involved in a great Mass and this Mass is our life and our death. That is, in prayer we offer our world to God, then God receives our offering by claiming it as his body and blood and the claim consecrates it. Such is Teilhard's understanding of Christian prayer. Having made this prayer we find our active life to be an extended act of communion, a communion that finally involves our death.

Basic to any understanding of Teilhard is his claim that Christ is the Soul of the World. The World Soul is an ancient, pre-Christian term that Teilhard, by appealing to St. Paul, would identify with the risen Christ. But Teilhard would modify the ancient understanding by seeing the world *in process* of gaining a soul. It is becoming increasingly more organically one. And evolution is the process by which things are becoming more unified so that the world will eventually form the body to which Christ is giving his Soul. So he would speak of a "Christogenesis." This process began ages ago and has led to the human; it is now for humans (with the grace of God) to continue the work by which the world becomes ever more animated by its single Soul. That is, we assist in preparing Christ's body, as Mary assisted in preparing his human body. Such is the value of human work.

When pressed to justify his claims, Teilhard appealed to St. Paul. The letters of St. Paul speak of the church as the body of Christ. The church, in order to separate this meaning from the Eucharist, identified the community of Christians as the *mystical* body of Christ. St. Paul said the church "makes bodily growth and upbuilds itself in love" (Eph 4:15). Following St. Paul, Teilhard would see love as the process by which things grow in coming together. Our work continues God's work, yet the growth itself is from God (Col 2:19). St. Paul never directly spoke of all creation as the body of Christ, but he use phrases suggesting the term *body of Christ* might be extended beyond the church to include all things. For he speaks of Christ as the one "in whom all things hold together" (Col 1:17; it is the soul that holds the elements of a living body together). And St. Paul told of a plan for the fullness of time when God "will unite all things in him, things in heaven and things on earth" The passage continues by saying God has made Christ "the head over *all things* for the church, which is his body, the fullness of him who fills all in all" (Eph 1:22–23). Just as Christ is head of the church, so he is the "head over all things," a phrase that suggests a wider sense of body that will include all creation so "that God may be everything to every one" (1 Cor 15:28)—much as our soul permeates our body; it is in all our members. This extension of the term *body* to the universe has not been common in Catholic theology. P. Benoit, O.P., would see in the latter Pauline epistles (Colossians and Ephesians—some believe these were written by a disciple of Paul) the term *body of Christ* extended to include "in an indirect fashion, the whole Cosmos";[9] but Benoit still had reservations. Teilhard would differentiate this body from the mystical body of Christ by calling it "the Cosmic Body of Christ."

The chapters that follow have different characters: the first is biographical; the second involves Teilhard's understanding of the scientific method; the third is scientific; the fourth is somewhat more difficult as it presents Teilhard's general philosophy as a context in which to understand his prayer; the fifth considers individual passages of Teilhard's "Mass"; the sixth considers adoration; and the seventh considers his apostolic dedication.

Since first reading Teilhard's "Mass on the World," I have met many others deeply affected by his writings; I have written books about him and have taught courses on his thought at Georgetown and elsewhere; I have talked with members of his family, with Jesuits and others who knew him well. They have helped in writing the present text. I mention in particular conversations with Pierre Leroy, S.J. (who worked with Teilhard many years in China), Rhoda de Terra (who tended Teilhard during his final years in New York), and Mary Wood Gilbert (a cousin of Lucile Swan and resident of Peking in the 1930s). Beyond these I have talked of Teilhard with Henri Cardinal de Lubac, S.J. (theologian friend of Teilhard); John McMahon, S.J. (New York Jesuit provincial during Teilhard's final days); Robert I. Gannon, S.J. (his rector during the same time); Jeanne Mortier (who arranged publication of Teilhard's manuscripts); Claire Taschdjian (office manager of the Peking Medical Union in the 1940s); Lita Osmundson (longtime president and director of research at the Wenner-Gren Foundation for Anthropological Research); and many others. They have told me personally of the man, the scientist, the friend, and the priest. To all of them I am grateful.

But beyond the somewhat academic text that follows, Teilhard wrote his "Mass on the World" as a prayer, and to be understood it should be used that way. He prayed the text daily when unable to offer Mass. To assist others in praying the text I offer an adaptation that could be used as a prayer service—perhaps as part of a program on Teilhard, or globalization, or ecology, and so forth. Teilhard would see his "Mass" telling of the "Extensions of the Eucharist"; by it he hoped to bring out the wider dimension of what occurs in every Mass—so I suggest a way that the text may be used together with a Mass, to extend the Mass without intruding on the Mass itself. I have often used it this way with my students here and abroad. The text ends with a brief suggestion of how one might pray as Teilhard did.

Notes

1. GM, 73.
2. Or, Vol. 32, No. 46, #8.
3. Ratzinger, 29.
4. S, 65.
5. W, 205.
6. HM, 217.
7. LMF, 196.
8. D, 136.
9. Quoted in Kropf, 151.

Professor Pierre Teilhard de Chardin,
the eminent French paleontologist, who, together with
Father Licent, discovered the traces of Old Stone-age man
in the Ordos desert.

Father Emile Licent, the great collector and founder of the
Huang Ho-Pai Ho Museum.

1.

TEILHARD AND THE PRIESTHOOD

"I thank you, my God, for having made me a priest."

Pierre Teilhard de Chardin was born in Sarcenat in Central France on May 1, 1881, the fourth of eleven children. His parents were part of the local gentry who hired English and German governesses to tend to the early education of their children. But "maman" taught them catechism, and from her Pierre developed a love of the Mass and a devotion to the heart of Christ, the "Sacred Heart." "Papa" was interested in natural history and took the children on long walks, teaching them to identify the plants, animals, and rocks of the region. The area about their country home has been called a "geologist's paradise," and Pierre soon was fascinated by the large cones of burned-out volcanos that could be seen from his front door.

When Pierre was about six or seven he began collecting scraps of iron, a wrench, shells from a firing range, an hexagonal bolt, and so forth. He tells of going by himself to contemplate his "God of Iron," for iron seemed so hard and durable. Upon discovering that iron rusts and can be scratched, he fell into childhood despair; he had to look elsewhere for what would endure, turning first to the rocks and then to the earth itself. This soon become a passion for the All *(le Tout)* that would run through his whole life. He would speak of approaching his scientific work as a "votary."[1] In the summers the family stayed at Sarcenat, where daily they gathered with the servants for evening prayer; at Clermont in the winters, the family would go to evening Benediction of the Sacrament at the twelfth-century church of Notre Dame du Port. Teilhard wrote, "I doubt that anyone on earth could be happier than I was at that time."

1

In 1892 his mother brought Pierre to the Jesuit boarding school of Mongre, near Villefranche-sur-Saone. There in the Chapel of the Sacred Heart he would make his first communion on the feast of the Ascension, May 26, 1892. Academically he did very well, winning twenty two scholastic awards, only one of which was in religion. Before graduating he wrote to his parents that he wanted to enter the Jesuit Order: "I believe God is calling me to leave the world." But when he returned home he looked so thin and exhausted that his father made him delay his entrance for a year. At home he continued his devotional life and studied math with a tutor. In March 1899, he entered the Jesuit novitiate at Aix-en-Provence.

Shortly after Teilhard took his vows as a Jesuit, Premier Emile Combe began enforcing French anticlerical laws that drove the Jesuits and most religious orders out of France. Teilhard was part of the rapid exodus, and continued his studies with other relocated Jesuits in Jersey, a British island off the French coast. There he studied mostly philosophy and the Latin and Greek classics; a colleague observed, "He could read Aeschylus like he was reading the newspaper." In 1904, Felix Pelletier, a Jesuit who had had professional training in chemistry and mineralogy, joined the community and soon they were spending days together climbing among the rocks of Jersey and speculating on the island's geology. Together they wrote an article on the minerals of Jersey.

In 1905 as part of his Jesuit training, Teilhard was sent to teach chemistry and physics at the Jesuit *college* (more or less equivalent to a U.S. high school) in Cairo. During his three years in Egypt he continued doing research and reported new finds back to Felix Pelletier; some previously unknown fossils now bear his name. "This was the East, I caught glimpses of it, and drank it in avidly, with no concern for its peoples and their history…but under the attraction of its light, its vegetation, its fauna and its deserts."[2] In August 1906 he made his annual retreat at Sidi Gaber on the Mediterranean coast near Alexandria. In his notes he indicated the attitude he wanted to maintain: "Perpetual Communion, the Eucharist and Will";[3] "Perpetual Communion" was an early statement of what would become a theme of his

"Mass on the World." At the same time, his interest in the earth continued to grow and left him in what he called a "somewhat muddled spiritual complex," for a passionate love for the All was smoldering within him and yet he remained determined to seek ordination as a Catholic priest. In 1908, following the ordinary course of Jesuit studies, he went to England to study theology at the French theologate now relocated at Hastings.

He was again with Felix Pelletier, and together they explored the countryside, finding significant fossils. One such exploration took them into an unfortunate venture. Six months after arriving at Hastings they met a local amateur geologist, Charles Dawson, who became the central figure in what is now known as the "Piltdown hoax." This refers to nine pieces of a human skull and the jawbone of an orangutan that were doctored to look ancient and as if they belonged to the same individual. On three occasions Teilhard assisted Dawson in digging at the site. In December 1912, Piltdown materials were presented to the scientific world and were widely acclaimed. They continued to fool anthropologists until 1953, when modern research techniques showed they had been artificially prepared. In 1980 Stephen Jay Gould, a Harvard anthropologist and TV personality, accused Teilhard of involvement in producing the fraud, a charge that has been abundantly refuted.* While at Hastings Teilhard read Henri Bergson's

---

* In his monthly column in *Natural History* for August 1980, Stephen Jay Gould accused Teilhard of complicity in preparing the hoax. Numerous scholars have taken issue with Gould: J. S. Weiner, who led in uncovering the fraud and later published *The Piltdown Forgery* (Oxford, 1955), claimed Dawson was the forger but allowed there might have been an accomplice. He had interviewed Teilhard in 1954 for about an hour. In 1981 Weiner spoke at Georgetown University, dismissing Gould's charge as "rubbish": "I had no reason then and I have no reason now—I have said so in public many times—to see in Teilhard a fellow conspirator" (a video of the talk is in the Georgetown University archives). Together with Weiner the present author has written a defense of Teilhard that appeared in *Teilhard & the Unity of Knowledge* (Paulist, 1983). Kenneth Oakley, Weiner's associate in uncovering the fraud, said the basis of Gould's charge is "completely untrue." Teilhard went with Dawson and Smith-Woodward on an early dig at Piltdown in June 1912 and twice again with Dawson in the summer of 1913. He was an early victim of the hoax, but not involved in preparing it. Many

Creative Evolution, a book he saw providing the fuel "for a fire that was already consuming my heart and mind."[4] The All he had known as smoldering in Egypt burst into flame, but, following Bergson, the All was seen to be *in process*. He told of the word *evolution* haunting his mind like a tune, like a summons held out to him. All things were evolving together, for one single life seemed to run through the natural world. The English countryside at sunset seemed to be charged with the same fossil life that he had been pursuing in rocky cliffs and quarries. "There were moments, indeed, when it seemed to me that a sort of universal being was about to take shape suddenly in Nature before my very eyes."[5]

Teilhard was ordained a subdeacon and a deacon in March 1911. Shortly before this ordination he wrote to his parents: "Through vows, a person really has the feeling of giving himself; through Orders, a person has to feel especially accepted."[6] This sequence of offertory and acceptance recurs later, constituting the offertory and consecration of his "Mass on the World."

Pierre's older sister, Francoise, had joined the Little Sisters of the Poor and had been serving the sick in Shanghai. As his priestly ordination approached she wrote to him: "Don't forget that I'm holding you to your promise to ask Our Lord at your first Mass that He deign to take me to Him completely and that He keep me in China until I die."[7] But before he could offer his first Mass, she had died of smallpox while tending those with the illness. He wrote to his distraught parents: "He [God] alone is the end of all things, so that when He takes someone to himself, it isn't to separate, but to unite. His will be done." As priestly ordination approached his parents sent him a chalice as an ordination

---

scholars have defended Teilhard's involvement as innocent; the best defense would seem to be articles by Tobias and Kennedy in *Current Anthropology* (June 1992 and February 1993). See also Charles Blinderman, *The Piltdown Inquest* (Prometheus, 1986) and John E. Walsh, *Unraveling Piltdown* (Random House, 1996). Recent evidence indicates Martin Hinton, a worker at the British Museum, prepared the fraud. The evidence is a trunk with Hinton's initials recently found in the museum attic containing fossils stained by the same complex process used on the Piltdown fossils (Nature, April 23, 1996). Nonetheless, Gould was a popular writer and has left an undeserved shadow on the name of Teilhard.

Teilhard and his family at the time of his ordination,
Hastings, 1911. From left to right: Pierre, Gonzague,
Joseph, his father, Victor, his mother.

gift; he sent them detailed instructions on travel to Hastings. They and four of his brothers were present on August 24, 1911, when he was ordained by Bishop Amigo of London, and they were present the following day as he offered his first Mass at the Church of Our Lady Star of the Sea. His younger brothers, Gabriel and Joseph, served the Mass, while Victor and Gonzague were in the congregation with his parents. As he continued his studies in theology, he went to parishes to assist with Masses and confessions. In December he had the academic honor of leading a Latin disputation on the Eucharist; afterward, he told his parents how it went: "Good, but not more striking than was necessary."[8]

In July 1912, Teilhard went to Paris to begin studies in paleontology under Marcellin Boule, a fellow Auvergnat and specialist in the Neanderthals. Boule was known to be anticlerical, but at their first meeting he and Teilhard began a good relationship and eventually Boule wanted Teilhard to replace him at the Paris Museum. Apart from his work in the laboratory, Teilhard traveled on many field trips about France, Spain, and Belgium with professional geologists. One instructor tells of a trip in the French Alps where he served Teilhard's Mass daily at 6:00 a.m.[9] Teilhard's scientific work was interrupted first by a period of Jesuit studies in spirituality and then more decisively by World War I: in December 1914 a draft board reviewed his case and found him "fit for duty." Two of his brothers were already at the front, as lieutenants in the artillery, and two others were in training to join them; the next to youngest had just been killed in action.[10] Shortly after Christmas Pierre entered the army and on January 22, 1915, was sent to the front as a stretcher bearer in a Moroccan regiment of Light Infantry and Zouaves. Soon, he was offered an appointment as chaplain with the rank of captain, but he refused: "Leave me among the men." Among the men he served as a corporal with a pack on his back, but unofficially he was their chaplain.

While Teilhard was at Hastings, he had been aware of a unity in the life evolving around him, feeling that at any moment the living world might appear as a single living Being. At that time humans did not fit into his picture, for each human seemed to constitute a world to one's self. But at the front he saw thousands of men acting with a single effort toward a single goal. "The 'Human-million,' with its psychic temperature and its internal energy, became for me a magnitude as evolutively, and therefore as biologically, real as a giant molecule of protein."[11] Now the fascinating All seemed to be focused in humanity. But this was not an abstract knowledge. Soldiers in wartime have felt strongly their common brotherhood, and so with Teilhard ("Leave me among the men"). He would retain vivid memories of how the troops shared in a collective passion and felt bonded to one another, "a sense of rising to a higher level of human existence."[12] Many years later, on seeing soldiers celebrating the end of World War II, he recalled his own wartime experience of unity and said there is "in the subsoil of humanity some mysteries of profound affinity which appear only fleetingly."[13] But "this perception of a natural psychic unity higher than our 'souls' requires, as I know from experience, a special quality and training in the observer."[14] During the war, his sense for the All, an "insatiable yearning for cosmic Organicity," became focused on the human. He would connect this organic All with what St. Paul had written of the body of Christ (a Pauline term telling of the Christian community and according to some theologians including all things). He would speak of Christ as Soul of the World, the one in whom all things hold together.[15]

In October 1915 Teilhard wrote to his cousin Marguerite telling her he was offering a spiritual form of the Mass, an early suggestion of what would become "The Mass on the World": "For the last three days I've been deprived of saying mass, and I don't know when I'll be able to say it again. I try to make up for it mentally (too infrequently and neglectfully, alas) performing the two fundamental acts of religion, offering and union, of which the mass is the most intimate expression of all."[16]

Wartime conditions were difficult. One account tells of the men improvising an altar and decorating it for Teilhard, using empty shells to serve as an altar bell. The soldiers were in daily peril and his priestly presence gave them much assurance. At times his unit was in an area without a priest and the local church was deserted or damaged in the war. He would open the rectory and church and return daily to offer Mass until his unit was trans-ferred elsewhere. He continued this ministry throughout his years in the military.[17] Once he offered Mass on the buffet of a bombed-out inn. On another occasion his unit was stationed in a swamp in Belgium; the ground was so marshy that the troops were unable to dig trenches, so to protect themselves they had constructed a three- or four-foot wall of sandbags, logs, and planks. An account of one of the soldiers reads:

> It was in one of these rat-infested shelters that Teilhard, upon the request of several Frenchmen with me, agreed to say a Mass for our families. This, if my memory serves, was at the beginning of January in 1916—about the 5th or 6th. Because it was impossible to stand upright in so low a structure, the celebrant had to say mass—and we to hear it—kneeling down; there were six of us there all told. As Teilhard was replacing in his little case the vessels and vestments he had used at Mass, the Germans sent a hail of shells down on our sector. Not a one of us was touched by the bursts; Teilhard in a calm and serious voice said, "I had still my blessing to give you. God being with us did not wish one of us to be hit." With that he gave us his blessing and returned to his aid post.[18]

On another occasion Teilhard wrote: "Yesterday, after a fortnight of not being able to say Mass, with so many friends to remember, with so many dangers safely avoided to thank for, and with the consciousness of the crying needs and bitter sorrows of the world, I said what was perhaps the most fervent Mass of my life."[19] At another time, he was able to offer daily benediction and delighted in the strong voices of the singers.

Between engagements, there were long stretches of silence and much time to think. In August 1915, he began keeping a journal-of-ideas, and the following April wrote the first of the essays that would make him famous, "Cosmic Life." There, he told of a communion with earth leading to a communion with God. It was his first systematic attempt to unite his feelings for the All with his Christian faith. The word *communion* was central to this unity, and it suggests the Mass. But the essay also speaks of "sacramental communion" bringing unity to the mystical body of Christ. (St. Paul likewise saw the Eucharist unifying the body of Christ: "Because there is one bread, we who are many are one body, for we all partake of the one bread" [1 Cor 10:17]) In the months that followed, he wrote additional essays. An essay written in 1917 would see the Eucharist sanctifying the cosmos: "Since first, Lord, you said, '*Hoc est corpus meum,*' not only the bread of the altar, but (to some degree) everything in the universe that nourishes the soul for the life of Spirit and Grace, has become *yours* and has become *divine*—it is divinized, divinizing, and divinizable."[20]

One of his wartime essays is an imaginative account of a military priest telling a friend of several visionary experiences; it evidently tells of himself. The setting is shortly before the battle at Douaumont and the priest recalls attending benediction. While gazing at the Host in the monstrance, the Host seemed to spread out beyond its limited contours. "It was as though a milky brightness were illuminating the universe from within, and everything were fashioned of the same kind of translucent flesh....through the mysterious expansion of the host the whole world had become incandescent, had itself become like a single giant host."[21] Then the immense Host, having purified and given life to everything, began to contract, drawing treasures into itself as benediction ended. The military priest then goes on to tell of another faith experience; he was carrying a pyx with a consecrated Host inside as he walked through the trenches visiting the troops. To feel closer to the Lord he pressed the pyx against his body, but a barrier of separation remained between himself and the Host. As the time came for him to receive communion, he prepared his heart, but even while receiving he found the separation remained. He decided this separation was the time he had yet to live, for perfect union could come only with death.[22] Perfect-union-only-with-death would become a major theme in "The Mass on the World." It is only beyond this life that our union with God can be complete. (At Douaumont today there is a battle memorial that includes a photo of a priest offering Mass before the battle. The priest is not identified, but many people see it as Teilhard—he was in the battle and had been the only priest in his regiment. Like Teilhard, the priest has a prominent nose and stands tall and erect; unlike Teilhard, he seems to have a receding chin.)

In June 1918, Teilhard made notations in his journal-of-ideas that suggest what he would call the extensions of the Eucharist: "The infinite circle of creatures is the total Host to consecrate. The crucible of their activities is the chalice to sanctify." Here he extends the meaning of priest: he observes that Christ is the only priest, "but each liberty has the final word for the divine invasion of one's own universe. Should this liberty be that of a priest, it operates throughout the Universe. The Sacramental consecration is haloed by a universal, analogical consecration."[23] He spoke of a special kind of priesthood that would "Christianize the organic and spiritual currents from which come forth the Body of Christ." He was near the Aisne

Teilhard offering Mass before the Battle of Douaumont,
October 1916

River with tall, straight trees arching above him and these suggested a Gothic cathedral: "You could not imagine a better temple of recollection."

In July he was again unable to offer Mass, so he wrote "The Priest," an extended prayer patterned on the Mass; it would develop later into his "Mass on the World." In this essay, he briefly indicates the difference between the "bread" (the growth) and the "wine" (the diminishments); in his "Mass on the World" the difference would become central. Over the positive developments, he would say, *"Hoc est corpus meum."* And over the suffering and loss, he would say, *"Hic est calix sanguinis mei."*[24] He ended with a statement of what the priesthood meant to him:

> Every priest, because he is a priest, has given his life to a work of universal salvation. If he is conscious of his dignity, he must no longer live for himself but for the world, as He lived whose anointed representative the priest is. I feel, Jesus, that this duty has a more immediate urgency for me, and a more exacting meaning, than it has for many others—far better men, too, than I....*To bring Christ, by virtue of a specifically organic connexion, to the heart of realities that are esteemed to be the most dangerous, the most unspiritual, the most pagan—in that you have my gospel and my mission....*
>
> *Because I am a priest*, I would henceforth be the first to become aware of what the world loves, pursues, suffers. I would be the first to seek, to sympathize, to toil: the first in self fulfilment, the first in self denial— I would be more widely human in my sympathies and more nobly terrestrial in my ambitions than any of the world's servants.

He noted the many grim battles wherein men close to him had been slaughtering one another for four years and asked, "Was there ever, my God, a humanity more like, in the shedding of its blood, to a sacrificed victim...more close, in its agony, to the supreme communion?" Death is the ultimate communion, and

An undated photo of Teilhard on expedition in China

the priest is the victim sacrificed; it is "the logical crowning of priesthood." So he called on fellow priests in the military to consecrate the sufferings around them as the blood of Christ. He was grateful for his own priesthood: "I thank you, my God, in that you have made me a priest—and a priest ordained *for War*."

Teilhard wrote many essays during his military service; nineteen have survived. He would look back fondly to his wartime years: "For me the War was a meeting with (an immersion in) the Absolute"; "The war marked the spring time of my ideas—my intellectual honeymoon."[25] In the years that followed he would refine, develop, and clarify his ideas, but they remained largely the same. He had come to see events around him, even the war, as part of a global evolution leading to a future fullness of Christ. But the front was also a great adventure that shaped his spirit. When apart from the actual fighting, he felt a nostalgia to return to where the action was. This desire to be in the action remained all his life. Max Begouen tells of him radiating a sense of peace to others, while "the curtains of machine-gun fire and the hail of bombardments both seemed to pass him by." Begouen continued,

I once asked Pere Teilhard, "What do you do to keep this sense of calm during the battle? It looks almost as if you don't see the danger and that fear does not touch you." He answered with that friendly smile that gave such a human warmth to his words, "If I'm killed I shall just change my state, that's all."[26]

With the end of the war he was demobilized in March 1919. He had served in battles at Ypres, Arras, Douaumont, Louvemont, and so forth; but he emerged from the war unscathed with two citations for bravery—the Croix de Guerre and the Medaille Militaire—and would be named a Chevalier in the Legion of Honor. From his army years, he retained a sense of adventure and seemed pleased to note that "a central element of faith is that it involves a risk."[27]

Teilhard resumed his studies at the Sorbonne and returned to the quiet of Jesuit life. But his wartime ideas began to circulate and he was invited to give talks; soon he was well known in the Catholic intellectual circles of Paris. The Eucharist was much on his mind. In an essay written in January 1920 he envisioned the beatitude of heaven as "a state of permanent eucharistic union" wherein the faithful remain one body. In a restricted sense, we have such a communion with one another now, but this does not interfere with our sacramental communions.[28] In the spring of 1922 he received his doctorate with honors from the Sorbonne and was elected president of the *Societé Géologique de France*.

It seemed he was about to begin a distinguished career in Paris as scientist and apostle, but a fellow Jesuit, Emile Licent, a scientist and missionary to China since 1914, had been finding quantities of interesting fossils. In 1922 he found tools of early humans in the Ordos Desert. He was skilled in dealing with the political troubles plaguing China at the time. Since 1919 he had been shipping materials back to the Paris Museum in large crates. Boule asked Teilhard to classify them, and Teilhard soon realized that for a proper appraisal he needed to visit the sites where they had been excavated; that meant a trip to China. His religious superiors approved. As he prepared to leave, a Belgian missionary warned Licent that soldiers in the Ordos were spreading rumors that foreign priests were in danger: "Recently, a certain Colonel Feng said that the country will have to be rid of us—that we are to be killed and our heads hung on the walls."[29] In spite of such warnings, in May 1923, with financial backing from the Paris Museum, Teilhard joined Licent in Tientsin and then traveled briefly to Peking to meet other scientists working in China. Returning to Tientsin, he and Licent left Tientsin by train on the morning of June 11 or 12 heading for the Ordos, a vast plateau in western Mongolia.

The main rail line brought them to Kalgan; on the following day "a primitive little train" spent fourteen hours bringing them to Bleu Ville (Kwei Ha Cheng); here they met with General Ma Fou Sion, a mandarin who controlled the whole area. They received his permission to cross the Yellow River and enter the Ordos; then another train brought them to the end of the rail line at Pao Tou. Licent had become fluent in Chinese and was a skillful negotiator; here he organized a party of ten mules, three donkeys, five mule-teers, two servants, and a military escort. But bandits and the drought made it unwise to go directly to the primary fossil site, the Sjara Osso Gol (a river that had cut deep gorges on the sides of which fossils were often exposed), so they headed west-northwest, a route that led them to important discoveries. At their digging sites they employed about twenty Chinese and Mongolian workers. Teilhard wrote, "There is no shade and no cool in the badlands," but the "torn naked earth" provided an incomparable field for their work. Another letter reads,

> I'm writing to you under canvas (it's raining!) from the most picturesque spot that exists: the bed of a deep ravine close to a Mongol dwelling scooped out in the middle of a table of hardened earth (cut through in the past by the Shara Uso Gol). All around are sand hills and steppes where the horses and sheep pasture beside gazelles, under the distant guard of the long-haired, big-booted Mongols.[30]

The few people living there dwelt in caves cut into the loess. The caravan grew to thirty animals carrying three tons of specimens. They discovered many ancient campsites, and in four months they had traveled more than six hundred miles beyond the rail line. The scientists loaded their findings on a rectangular barge, paid their workers, and drifted down the Hwang Ho (Yellow River) to Pao t'eou. On October 3, Teilhard wrote, "I am writing to you from the middle of the Hwang-Ho under a fairly comfortable tent pitched in the middle of a deep square boat which is whirling and drifting downstream rather like a tub....Our booty is piled up on board (sixty cases = 3,000 kilos)."[31] The river journey lasted ten days; then at Pao t'eou they loaded their findings on a train and began the ride back to Tientsin, where they arrived on October 11.[32]

"The Mass on the World" was written during this expedition, for the text begins with a reference to being "in the steppes of Asia" and ends with the note, "Ordos, 1923." But it is not that simple. Ever since writing "The Priest" (1918), Teilhard had been reworking his text and sharing it with others. On August 7, 1923, he wrote from the Ordos to a friend in Paris, "As I travel on mule back for whole days on end, I repeat, as in the past—for lack of any other Mass—the 'Mass on the World,' which you already know, and I believe I can say it with still greater clarity and conviction than before."[33] Later that month, he wrote to another friend, "I keep developing, and slightly improving, with the help of prayer, 'My Mass on Things.'"[34] Both letters imply that his friends in Paris knew an earlier version of the work; this might have been "The Priest," but there is reason to suspect he had already been revising the essay before leaving for China. He was in the Ordos for about ten days on his way south and then returned to it for twenty-four days at the Sjara Osso Gol, "a curious little stream" at the base of a 250-foot canyon. Otherwise they spent much time digging to the north, the west, and especially the south of the Ordos. Near to where they were digging, there were tabular earth mounds and on these they offered Mass. Perhaps this inspired Teilhard to speak of his Mass on the "Altar of the World." There was a mission station of the Belgian missionaries not too far away. On the feast of the Assumption (August 15), they joined the Belgian fathers in a procession of the Eucharist proceeded by Mongol horsemen bearing savage banners and beating gongs.[35] Unfortunately, during this expedition Teilhard did not bring his journal-of-ideas, for it has no entry from June 11 to October 15—several days after his return.

In Tientsin, Teilhard spent much time identifying the fossils they had found, and many of the better ones were sent back to the Paris Museum according to the arrangements by which the expedition was financed. Yet his "Mass" was much on his mind: he noted in his journal, "Each communion, each consecration is a notch further in our incorporation into Christ."[36] Teilhard knew he and Licent had made significant finds in locating early campsites and tools, but they had not found any old human bones, so he decided to remain in China until the following September and return to the Ordos. He wrote to Boule at the Museum (asking for further support) and to Mgr. Baudrillart at the Institut Catholique (asking for an extended absence from teaching). Both supported his decision for another season in China.

In March 1924, he wrote an essay, "Mon Universe" (his second essay with this title). This contains his most complete account of the "extensions of the Eucharistic Presence":

> We must say that the initial Body of Christ, his *primary body*, is confined to the species of bread and wine. Can Christ, however, remain contained in this primary Body? Clearly, he cannot. Since he is above all omega, that is, the universal "form" of the world, he can obtain his organic balance and plenitude only by mystically assimilating (and we have already explained the hyperphysical sense to be attached to that word) all that surrounds him. The Host is like a blazing hearth from which flames spread their radiance. Just as the spark that falls into the heather is soon surrounded by a wide circle of fire, so, in the course of centuries, the sacramental host—for there is but one Host, ever growing greater in the hands of a long succession of priests—the

Host of bread, I mean, is continually being encircled more closely by another, infinitely larger, Host, which is nothing but the universe itself—the universe gradually being absorbed by the universal element. Thus when the phrase *"Hoc est Corpus meum"* is being pronounced, *"hoc"* means *"primario"* the bread; but *"secondario,"* in a second phase occurring in nature, the matter of the sacrament is the world, through which there spreads, so to complete itself, the superhuman presence of the universal Christ. The world is the final, and the real, Host into which Christ gradually descends, until his time is fulfilled. Since all time a single word and a single act have been filling the universality of things: *"Hoc est Corpus meum."* Nothing is at work in creation except in order to assist, from near at hand or from afar, in the consecration of the universe.[37]

When he heard of a Eucharistic Congress being held in Chicago, he wrote, "I follow with a profound interest these grand collective manifestations. But was there among those thousands of adorers one sole preacher to try to explain the true extensions of the Eucharist and its animating place in human work? To transform Catholics it would be enough to show them what to communicate and sympathize mean in their fullness." Beyond transforming Catholics, he wrote to a non-Christian friend: "If you only knew how I would like to have been for ten minutes in the Chicago stadium to shout to the crowd what it is to 'communicate' and to 'sympathize.'"[38]

In speaking of the extensions of the Eucharist, Henri de Lubac, a Jesuit friend of Teilhard and a scholar of early church writings, would see Teilhard spontaneously rediscovering "something of the fullness of tradition that our age was by way of forgetting."[39] As March ended, Teilhard wrote a journal entry wondering about the role of religious rites (the Mass properly speaking); he was concerned lest they set up a new body and not animate the body (the universe) that already exists. "Does the Church have need of a Body other than the cosmos?" He answers by another

Teilhard in India, 1924

question, "Would not the large Host attenuate itself if there was not the host of bread to render it real (in symbolizing it)?"[40]

In April 1924, Teilhard and Licent set out for their second expedition; this time they went to the Gobi—north of the Ordos. They headed into the steppes ten days by camel and mule north of Kalgan. "We shall be six weeks without any communication with the civilized world, but work will keep me from feeling isolated." He told of climbing a grassy hill marked by a heap of stones that the Mongols called an obo—for them, it served as both altar and landmark; the devout Mongol would add a stone to it as he passed. At one obo the local people had added three poles: "Standing there, I offered up the world of Mongolia to Christ, whose name no man has ever invoked in that place."[41] Such an invocation resembled the offertory of his "Mass." The expedition of 1924 was not as successful with either new essays or new fossils as was the earlier one. In September he was able to visit his sister's grave in Shanghai and from there return to Paris.

Teilhard brought back forty crates of material for the Paris Museum. He was working through these when a letter came from his Jesuit provincial expressing concern about an essay he had written on original sin before he left for China: "Note on Some Possible Historical Representations of Original Sin."[42] In the essay Teilhard sees the story of Adam and Eve as a parable of the human condition and not a historical account of human origins. This is a common opinion among theologians today, but it was not so common eighty years ago. He also argued that humans came from more than a single couple. He had written the essay for other theologians and did not intend it for publication. But, during his stay in China, the essay was removed from his desk at the Institut Catholique and sent to the Holy Office in Rome. Teilhard was summoned to his provincial's office in Lyons and asked to sign a formal promise that he would never again write anything contrary to the Church's traditional position. After attempts to change some of the wording and much personal anguish, he signed the statement during his retreat in 1925. He agreed to six propositions, but what they said is no longer known;[43] signing them involved months of anguish and uncertainty. He picked up an image from his "Mass" to explain his actions: "Yes, I believe that I will communicate with a profound joy from this small chalice." But, hoping he had not compromised his integrity, he added, "I would like to be certain, at least, that it is the blood of Christ."[44] In the meantime, Teilhard was becoming increasingly well known in Paris by giving scientific talks and preaching retreats. After one three-day retreat, a retreatant said:

> Activity on the human level—work in the world—was presented to us as the most immediate realization of God's will, the extensions of his most central designs for the world. The dovetailing of all this with the most exacting spiritual ideals, and with the most deeply personal love of Jesus Christ, was for me, and for many of us, a great awakening.[45]

Teilhard visited his old theologate at Hastings and found the Jesuit seminarians so enthused about his ideas that he was kept talking six hours per day. Church authorities were not pleased when they heard of his influence and made it increasingly difficult for him to continue his work in Paris.

Beyond agreeing to the six propositions, Teilhard was required to renounce his teaching position at the Institut Catholique and needed Vatican approval to publish any future writings in philosophy or theology. No restrictions were ever placed on his scientific writings. Through this crisis and others that followed, he was supported by Jesuit friends and other theologians who agreed with him. Since he had gained a large popular following, his religious superiors were relieved when in the spring of 1926 he set out again for China. There he would continue his fieldwork and write, "My most active moments are still when I am saying my 'Mass upon the altar of the world,' to divinize the new day."[46] And on another expedition: "During eight weeks when I had to live without the sacraments, I never ceased to communicate with a sort of calm exhilaration for the Sacrament of life animated by God."[47]

The Chou-Kou-Tien team in China, 1929: Barbour, Teilhard, Black, visitor, Young, two students, Pei.

In the years that followed Teilhard kept working on his "Mass." In 1926 he considered writing a new version; this eventually resulted in *The Divine Milieu*. Though this work includes many references to the Mass, his general intent had changed. Still many passages speak of the Eucharist: "There is only one Mass, one Communion, Christ died once in agony." And in "the eucharist Christ controls...the whole movement of the universe." "As our humanity assimilates the material world, and as the Host assimilates our humanity, the eucharistic transformation goes beyond and completes the transubstantiation of the bread on the altar." "In a true sense, the sacramental species are formed by the totality of the world, and the duration of the creation is the time needed for its consecration."[48]

In the summer of 1929 he wrote "from an inn in the depths of the Shansi":

> In the last two months I have again started to live that life (familiar to me since the war) in which my most substantial spiritual nourishment (with a real Mass at infrequent intervals) lies in the mental Mass "on the World" that I have often spoken to you about and at which you are always present. I am ceaselessly deepening and working over that Mass. If I get time this autumn I'll set it down in its nth form. I rather feel it is now reaching whatever degree of perfection I'm capable of giving it.[49]

Yet in the same year, he began "thinking of a third draft, considerably fuller." This would be "more mature" and would be titled *The Sacrament of the World*,[50] a work never written.

Teilhard was restricted in what he could do in Paris, but from time to time he was allowed to return there in connection with his scientific work and visit family and friends. After one such visit in 1928, he arranged an African visit with a friend, adventurer, and amateur anthropologist, Henri de Montfried. On Christmas Eve he offered midnight Mass in a Capuchin chapel in Ethiopia. The chapel smelled of earth and the altar was covered with a zebra skin; the local people, the Danakils, gathered around with their weapons in hand watching the proceedings in awe.[51] The following day, De Montfried returned to his home and Teilhard went on to explore some recently discovered ancient cave art; the cave was filled with giant cave wasps that left him recovering from their stings as he resumed his trip to Asia.

Upon returning to China, Teilhard was put in charge of classifying the fossils that came from Chou kou tien, a large excavation southwest of Peking. The overall director of the work was Davidson Black. In early December 1929, as the diggers were closing down for the winter, a Chinese archeologist came upon a skull embedded in rock. Diggers broke free a large section of rock including the skull, wrapped the rock and skull in old laundry to conceal it from bandits, and hurried it back to Peking. There it became known as Peking Man and word of the find spread quickly, catching the imagination of the world. Teilhard was already known in scientific circles for his articles on the geology of Asia, but his reputation increased considerably with his accounts of Peking Man. He claimed Peking Man made tools and identified them as the earliest humans to domesticate fire (it is now known fire was domesticated earlier). These materials were about 400,000 years old. A second important skull was found at the site in the summer of 1930 and Teilhard's scientific reputation continued to advance. He traveled widely, attending geological conferences and lecturing at universities in Europe and the United States.

In 1930 he joined the American adventurer, Roy Chapman Andrews, on a trip into the Gobi (north of the Ordos). In his official account of the trip, Andrews wrote, "We were delighted to have Pere Teilhard as a colleague, for his brilliant achievements and charming personality endeared him to all of us."[52] Andrews tells how he located for them a rich fossil bed. In 1931 Teilhard was the geologist on an expedition across Asia, the Crossiere Jaune, a trip sponsored by the Citroen Corporation to advertise their cars and trucks. He was the only practicing Catholic on the expedition, which limited his priestly work. But on New Year's Day 1932, he celebrated Mass at a mission station at Liang-chow, and all those on the expedition attended. A copy of his sermon remains:

> What we ask of that universal presence which envelops us all, is first to reunite us, as in a shared, living centre with those whom we love, those who are so far away from us here, are themselves beginning this same new year. Then considering what must be the boundless power of this force, we beseech it to take a favorable hand for us and for our friends and families....Around us and in us, God, through his deep-reaching power, can bring all this about. And it is in order that he may indeed do so that, for all of you, I am about to offer him this Mass, the highest form of Christian prayer.[53]

The expedition gave him a cursory look at much of the geology of Asia, and soon he was part of a smaller expedition nearer to Peking. Jia Lanpo, a Chinese archeologist, was twenty three when he first met Teilhard and recalled, "This scientist of towering stature quickly put me at ease with his amicable manner and his patience and tirelessness in educating the young learner." "It was a moving experience to see how many hardships the man could bear."[54] He endured floods and blizzards, bad food and no food, insects, snakes, wasps, scorpions, bandits, arrests, and civil war, and through it all he was known as "the smiling scientist." As the years went on he would do fieldwork in India, Burma, and Java with Helmut de Terra, who wrote of him, "He was devoid of the professional jealousies which so often insinuate themselves into professional circles....He never insisted on being accorded the privileges to which his status as the guest and senior member of our party really entitled him."[55] All the while he continued writing scientific articles, sometimes stretching the meaning of "science" in an attempt to get them published. His scientific writings have been collected in ten large volumes, *L'Oeuvre scientifique*. He kept writing philosophic and religious essays, some of which were privately printed in China and others stenciled and privately circulated among friends. These are now collected in thirteen volumes, and a dozen collections of his letters have been published.

While working in China he developed a friendship with Lucile Swan, an American artist who came to Peking to study Chinese sculpture. She was taken with him and his ideas. In her journal she wrote: "I love you every minute of every day….I love you so much it hurts, but that is probably not the way you want me to love you."[56] She worked with him as he developed his ideas, but had difficulty understanding his chastity, for chastity did not seem to be a part of evolution; so to clarify his ideas for himself and for her, he wrote an essay called, "The Evolution of Chastity."[57] In a general way, the essay tells of "platonic friendships" and ends with his most quoted line: "Someday when men have conquered the winds, the waves, the tides and gravity, they will harness for God the energies of love; and then, for the second time in the history of the world, man will have discovered fire." As his problems with the Church increased and difficulties continued with his Jesuit superiors in China, she could not understand his continued fidelity to either the Church or the Jesuits. So in January 1937 he wrote a long letter to her in English explaining his life: "Above all, have no doubt, that I do all I can to be loyally a 'priest' in the full meaning of the word. I say my mass and I follow to the best of my ability the rules of my Order. In the interior of which I am considered as a 'good *religieux*' and even perhaps a bit more."[58] He then tells of his passion for the earth and says that with the passing of time this passion will become more general until it requires a profound change in the understanding of Christian life, but not a deformation. "It will be the same current of living love for the same living reality (the Christ) which will continue over us."[59]

In being "loyally a 'priest,'" Teilhard was faithful in saying his breviary. Etienne Gilson tells of attending a philosophical conference and there seeing Teilhard "completely oblivious of what was going on around him and absorbed in the reading of his breviary."[60] George Barbour, a fellow scientist who worked with Teilhard on many expeditions, tells how he would set out to do fieldwork with his breviary in the left upper pocket of his jacket.

Teilhard in the Western Hills of Peking, 1940

During work he would take it out, read the office of the day, and then sit in silence.[61] On one occasion a temperamental mule kicked Teilhard on the head, and soon a blood blister the size of a pigeon egg developed. Throughout the night Barbour kept Teilhard's temple cool by constantly changing compresses. A devout Presbyterian, he read aloud to Teilhard in Latin the office of the day from Teilhard's breviary.[62]

Teilhard had written mostly essays, but in the fall of 1938 he decided to write a comprehensive account of his understanding of evolution; it would show the central place of humanity in the whole process and lead to a Soul at the center of humanity that he identified as the Omega Point. He would call the work *Le Phenomene humain*. In writing it he was sensitive to the objections the Church had raised and hoped to get Church approval. Writing was interrupted by travels to America and Europe as the latter was preparing for World War II. While in Paris he met a woman, Jeanne Mortier, who had been deeply impressed in reading a mimeographed copy of *Le Milieu Divin* (mimeographed as this did not violate the injunction not to have his works *printed*);

she felt delivered from the constrictions of her previous studies in scholastic theology. She attended one of his scientific lectures and afterward asked to see him. They had several meetings and soon she was volunteering to serve as his secretary and arrange his papers. She tells of being present on one occasion as he said Mass:

> Not having yet read his "Mass on the World," I was seized by the concentration with which Father celebrated. One sensed he was in a *tete a tete* with God. He truly offered Him the Universe, consecrated it in his personal consecration, communicated with it in his communion, The sobriety of his gestures, the gravity of his expression indicating the total consciousness that he had of his priesthood and of the God who was present to him.[63]

Others were likewise impressed: the wife of the French ambassador to Tokyo, Mme. Arsene-Henry, said, "Whoever has not seen Teilhard say Mass has seen nothing."[64] Teilhard was active with the students from the Ecole Normale when he was in Paris. One of them tells about hesitating between the Catholicism in which he was raised and the secular values of the school. In listening to Teilhard, the supernatural suddenly became real to him: "I discovered that the Mass is an action which changes the world, and felt the overpowering reality of the Christian fact."[65] One of Teilhard's biographers tells of having on hand several private testimonies of priests he brought back to the faith.[66]

Teilhard left Mlle. Mortier copies of many of his essays, and after his return to China she began reproducing and circulating them; he would write to her suggesting additional places to send them. One letter speaks of having 320 stenciled copies made of several essays.[67] Both she and he contributed to the expense.

In September 1939, Teilhard returned to China just as World War II broke out in Europe. He continued to see Lucile Swan, and the friendship had good moments and troubled moments. After one difficult evening, she wrote him a letter that it seems she did not mail:

What happens to cause this deep feeling of depression and outbursts like yesterday? It is true that things have not changed, at least your attitude has not changed. It is just that I understand it better....But Pierre, I do appreciate you and I do believe that you have something really important to give man and if there is anyway that I can help I really do want to do it...It is when I want some human, some warm response from you and day after day it does not come—then that terrible feeling of aloneness and losing you gets more than I can stand—and then I realize that I am not losing anything, because I never had it.[68]

Soon Teilhard became intently involved in writing *Le Phénomene humain.* He would work on it daily and bring what he had written to discuss with Lucile. She made many suggestions, most of which he did not accept; yet she was flattered when he would refer to it as "our work." He finished it on June 18, 1940, the very day France surrendered to the German Blitzkrieg. The work has an optimistic conclusion, but in writing it Teilhard was overcome with grief. He sent one copy to the United States and one to France as precautions lest the work be lost.

In 1941 it seemed increasingly evident that the United States would go to war with Japan and Americans were strongly advised to leave China; in August, Lucile returned to the United States. As a Frenchman, Teilhard was not in the same situation (the Vichy government was allied with Germany). At the time he was living with two other Jesuits on the grounds of the French embassy. For safekeeping, the skulls and other bones of Peking Man were packed for shipment to the United States. They were taken to the U.S. embassy in early December, but in the confusion that followed the bombing of Pearl Harbor the Japanese over-ran the American military base and the skulls and other bones of Peking Man were lost. The woman who packed the skulls for shipping suggests the Japanese probably thought they were someone's family bones being sent home for burial, and they dumped them into the China Sea. The Japanese were intent on finding the Peking skulls and ransacked the Peking Medical Union looking for them without success; in their anger they dumped the other materials out on the street. But all of it was retrieved.

During the years of World War II, Teilhard's ability to travel was greatly restricted; often he was unable to leave a small area around the foreign legations. There he continued working with the many fossils already collected. He established a regular routine that would begin with morning Mass at 7:00 and breakfast with Pierre Leroy (a fellow Jesuit) at 8:00; after a brief conversation, he would go to work in his laboratory. In the evenings he would often visit friends with Pierre Leroy.[69] He became the center of a small circle of friends whom he encouraged by optimistic accounts of the new world that would follow the war. But personally he was often overcome by depression. Life was austere, still he could joke, "Where I live we have no problem with mice, for there's nothing to eat." In 1944 he wrote an "Introduction to the Christian Life" that included a reflection on the Eucharist:

> Consider…what happens when we go to communion.
>
> In the first place, and immediately, we enter personally into physiological contact, at the moment of communion, with the assimilative power of the incarnate Word. What is more, however, this particular contact—our *nth* communion, say—does not follow on discontinuously from the *n* communions which preceded it in our life; it combines organically with the earlier communions in the unity of a single spiritual development, co-extensive with the whole duration of our life. All the communions of our life are, in fact, only successive instants or episodes in one single communion—in one and the same process of Christification.[70]

In August 1945 the Japanese surrendered to the United States, but it was not until December that the U.S. Marines arrived in Peking, and the American radios kept asking, "Where is Fr. Teilhard? Where is Sinanthropus [the remains of Peking Man]?" There were rumors that Teilhard had been killed in Tibet, but he had been confined to the area around Peking. After the liberation, Teilhard still had difficulties in arranging travel to Paris and did not arrive there until May 3, 1946. In his absence, Mlle. Mortier had been multiplying copies of his writings and sending them to an ever larger circle of admirers. He found himself a minor celebrity and soon was occupied with lectures, retreats, visits, and phone calls; foreign invitations came from Belgium, Switzerland, and Italy. He believed the time had come for his vision to be accepted. But on the last night of May 1947, he had a major cardiac infarction and was rushed to a hospital where he hovered between life and death for ten days. Doctors ordered six months of quiet. Gradually he was able to resume his work, but after this crisis he would always be limited by his health. His bouts of depression became more severe. Hoping to get approval to publish *The Phenomenon of Man* and accept a Chair offered to him at the College de France, he went to Rome in the fall of 1948. There, he reworked *Le Phénomene humain* with the Roman censors in mind and added explanatory passages. But he returned to Paris without success: both requests were refused.

Teilhard's ideas had become highly popular in Catholic intellectual circles in Paris but were an embarrassment to Church authorities, so they forbade him to give large public addresses; one account tells of his coming to speak and, upon finding a large audience waiting, he refused to speak. Rumors had it that the French bishops were about to make a new complaint about him to Rome. "I feel the moment has come for me to disappear for a time from Paris, where things are getting 'too hot' for me personally. For the past six months the press has been speaking too much about me and my indiscretions."

Teilhard needed "a shelter outside of France." In the past, he could return to his work in China, but now the Communists were in control and were not receiving foreign clergy. But he long had an interest in going to South Africa, where early pre-human fossils had been found near Johannesburg. So Teilhard wrote to Paul Fejos of the Wenner-Gren Foundation in New York asking him to sponsor a trip to South Africa. Fejos approved and, in 1951, limited by his heart problems and nervous anxiety, he prepared to travel to the African sites and, with the approval of his religious superiors, he was accompanied by an American woman, Rhoda de Terra (the divorced wife of Helmut de Terra—a companion of Teilhard on many digs), who made all the travel arrangements. Many Jesuits in Paris were concerned lest Teilhard die on the voyage, and they would not be able to publish his religious writings. So three days before his departure, his Jesuit superior, having consulted a canon lawyer, found that Teilhard could bequeath his manuscripts to someone outside of the Society. Jeanne Mortier was the obvious choice, so, when she came on a farewell visit, he turned his papers over to her.

He arrived in Cape Town in late July and took the night train across the Transvaal to Johannesburg. He felt invigorated to be working in the field again. In seeing the fossils and excavation sites in Africa and in talking with local scientists, Teilhard concluded that the human species had originated in Africa, not Asia as was then generally believed. He also concluded that the Australopithecine remains found there were not directly on the human line. He wrote to Jeanne Mortier: "I take up again, my 'Mass on the World,'" and, "Each day I make several deepenings or clarifications."[71] Soon he was wondering if he should just leave it alone.

Teilhard had been advised it would be wise to write to the Jesuit general in Rome explaining where he stood. So in leaving South Africa, he wrote to the general asking him to take him as he was—a man dominated by a feeling of the organic realness of the world. He spoke of a progression of all things into Xristo Jesu, saying this was the only atmosphere in which he could breathe, worship, and believe. "What might have been taken as my attitude during the last thirty years for obstinacy or disrespect, is simply the result of my absolute inability to contain my own feeling of wonderment." He added that he felt "more indissolubly bound to the hierarchical Church and to the Christ of the Gospel than ever before in [his] life."[72] As the letter ends, he tells the general that the Wenner-Gren Foundation that supported his work in Africa wanted him to prolong his stay with them in New York. Many

French Jesuits and Church authorities were relieved that he was no longer in Paris.

His notes for a retreat made in June 1952 speak again of writing a new version of his "Mass." He turned to the final pages of his journal-of-ideas and began making notations for the new text; these included drawings showing converging arrows ascending for the offertory and diverging arrows descending for the consecration. He often mentioned that he was working on a new version, but no traces of it remain. Mlle. Mortier affirmed that she was given only a single text. It has no alterations or markings in the margins.

In New York Teilhard stayed at St. Ignatius' Rectory on Park Avenue, only a fifteen-minute walk to the Wenner-Gren, where he had a small office on the top floor. On some days he walked across Central Park to work in the library of the Museum of Natural History. Soon he had settled into a routine of rising for daily meditation at 5:00 a.m., saying his Mass, taking breakfast, and arriving at the Wenner-Gren by 8:00.[73] Years later the New York Provincial remembered how simply he made his manifestation of conscience. Fejos was glad to have a "dreamer" as a research associate, a scientist who was willing to consider the larger human issues. In November 1952, Teilhard wrote to Mlle. Mortier asking her to send him a copy of the "Mass on the World," as he wanted to rewrite it with a different tone.[74] In 1953, the Wenner-Gren Foundation sponsored a second trip to South Africa to help them decide which proposed excavations they should sponsor. "I am once more not exactly in the field, but in close contact with old mother Earth; and you know that, for me, there is no better way of rejuvenation, and even 'adoration.'"[75] Again Rhoda de Terra made travel arrangements and accompanied him—while Lucile Swan was hurt by his continued attention to Rhoda. He visited excavations in Rhodesia before returning to New York by way of Rio and Trinidad.

In March 1954 large-scale renovations were begun at the Jesuit residence (St. Ignatius Church, Regis and Loyola schools) and all the Jesuits not directly attached to the parish or schools were asked to relocate to other Jesuit houses. It was suggested that

Teilhard live at Fordham in the Bronx. But aware of his limited health, the Jesuit provincial, John McMahon, gave him and another French Jesuit, Father de Breuvery, permission to live at the Lotos Club on East 66th Street; Teilhard noted the place was "rigorously cloistered." Here he was near the Wenner-Gren Foundation on 71st Street, and a five-minute walk to the Dominican Church of St. Vincent Ferrer. In 1999 the Dominicans posted a plaque: "At this altar Pierre Teilhard de Chardin of the Society of Jesus regularly celebrated the Eucharist in the final year of his life, 1954–55."

In 1954 he was allowed to return to France to visit friends and fellow scientists. Rhoda de Terra again made arrangements and accompanied him. He suffered from nervous anxiety and she, more than anyone else, was able to calm his nerves. She had little interest in philosophy or religion ("He wanted a mother, so I mothered him"), but she often heard him speak of the Mass and asked to attend; Teilhard always refused. However, while traveling with him in France together with Fr. Leroy and a driver, they stopped at a small country church where she was proud to attend his Mass: "I was in the audience." In Paris he again was a celebrity and Jesuit superiors became nervous about his presence and asked him to leave earlier than he had planned. He went to England to visit friends and scientific associates. There he recounted his memories of Piltdown (the story of fraud had broken seven months earlier) and soon returned to New York greatly discouraged and again suffering from nervous depression.

In 1955, a few weeks before his death, he wrote a final account of his faith, "The Christic." There he told again of "the words of the Consecration [being] applied not only to the sacrificial bread and wine but, mark you, to the whole mass of joys and sufferings produced by the Convergence of the World as it progresses."[76]

On Holy Thursday, April 7, Teilhard wrote in his journal a brief statement of his faith: "The two articles of my creed: The universe is centered and Christ is its center." He cited three verses of St. Paul that end "that God may be all in all" (1 Cor 15:26–28). On Holy Saturday he and Fr. de Breuvery heard one another's confession; on Easter Sunday he said his private Mass, had break-fast, and went to St. Patrick's Cathedral for a high Mass. Afterward he joined Rhoda de Terra and her daughter for a concert and, as he was not feeling well, they left early and went to the de Terras for Easter dinner. As dinner was being prepared he fell full length on the floor and was dead within minutes from a cerebral hemorrhage. On Easter Monday his body was laid out in the chapel of the Jesuit residence on Park Avenue; he was in his priestly vestments, with a crucifix and a rosary in his hands. On Easter Tuesday his funeral Mass was held at St. Ignatius' Church, and only a handful of people were present. The body was taken ninety miles north for burial at the Jesuit cemetery in Poughkeepsie, New York. The soil was wet with spring rains and they could not dig the grave for several days. Today the Jesuit property around the cemetery has been sold to the American Culinary Institute, but the cemetery is still owned by the Jesuits. Those at the Culinary Institute say that almost every day someone asks to visit his grave.

Many years before his death Teilhard spoke of death as the great moment of communion. In *The Divine Milieu*, this was his prayer:

> Because, of the two of us, you are infinitely the stronger, it is on you that falls the part of consuming me in the union that should weld us together. Vouchsafe, therefore, something more precious still than the grace for which all the faithful pray. It is not enough that I should die while communicating. Teach me to treat my death as an act of communion.[77]

No one knew Teilhard as did his cousin Marguerite. She arranged for the publication of the wartime letters she had received from him, adding a brief introduction. She wrote that during the war "he was, as he would be all his life, a priest first and foremost."[78] Claude Cuenot also knew Teilhard well. He wrote a life of Teilhard with emphasis on his scientific work. But in ending his study he wrote, "To the very core of his being, Teilhard was a priest."[79] I have known Teilhard only by his writings and what others have told me. But his "Mass" has so deeply affected my own that I think of him primarily as a priest.

Notes

1. HM, 198.
2. HM, 23.
3. Nr, 352.
4. HM, 25.
5. HM, 26.
6. LH, 138.
7. LH, 152.
8. LH, 179.
9. LGI, 19.
10. MM, 24.
11. HM, 31.
12. F, 22.
13. UL, JTdC; December 10, 1945.
14. HE, 118.
15. Col 1:17.
16. MM, 75.
17. MM, 30–31, 114.
18. Cuenot, 26.
19. MM, 120.
20. W, 146.
21. HU, 49.
22. HU, 53.
23. J, 328–29.
24. W, 208–10.
25. Nr, 57; LLZ, 52.
26. Corte, 15.
27. Nr, 91.
28. C, 16–17.
29. Cuenot, 48.
30. LLZ, 51.
31. LLZ, 55.

32. Barbour, 27.
33. LLZ, 52.
34. LT, 86; note alternate title.
35. Lukas, 82.
36. J, February 27, 1924.
37. S, 65–66.
38. LTF, 40.
39. De Lubac, RT, 76.
40. UJ, March 31, 1924.
41. LT, 119.
42. See C, 45–55.
43. Li, 123.
44. Li, 118.
45. Quoted in Cuenot, 60.
46. LT, 140.
47. UL, E. LeRoy, August 9, 1926.
48. D, 125.
49. LLZ, 94.
50. Li, 199.
51. Lukas, 108.
52. Andrews, 422.
53. Cuenot, 133–34.
54. Jia, 249, 250.
55. DeTerra, 52.
56. LS, 18–19.
57. T, 60–87.
58. LS, 65.
59. LS, 67.
60. Cuenot, 224.
61. Barbour, 33, 34.
62. Barbour, 104.
63. LJM, 13.
64. Cuenot, 258.
65. Cuenot, 88.
66. Cuenot, 106.
67. LJM, 61.
68. LS, 139–40.
69. Cuenot, 257.

70. C, 166.
71. LJM, 80, 81.
72. D, 38–40.
73. Lukas, 360.
74. LJM, 119.
75. LS, 285.
76. HM, 94.
77. D, 90.
78. MM, 31.
79. Cuenot, 385.

2.

THE TRANSFORMATION
OF THE WORLD IN SCIENCE
AND IN THE MASS

"Scientists are Priests."

Teilhard gained a considerable scientific reputation through his work in geology and human evolution. So he spoke as an authority on evolution when he claimed the process was leading to the formation of the body of Christ. He stated it briefly: "Fundamentally—since all time and for ever—but one single thing is being made in creation: the body of Christ."[1] This body will eventually unite all things in an organic union of which Christ will be the Soul. But, as with any organism, the elements would not lose their individual character, they would become more deeply themselves. He expressed this in a brief phrase: "union differentiates."

Thus, in an organic union, as in a human body, each organ (e.g., the heart, the liver, etc.) can be fully itself only when it is united to the organism. Integrated into the wider organism its own identity is enhanced, not eliminated: union differentiates. But such a union can be found in other contexts: when two people unite in love, they feel united with one another and at the same time feel they have finally become themselves, more individualized than ever. "Union differentiates" can also be found in knowledge: when a hypothesis unites a large mass of data, the details seem to stand out more sharply than ever. This enhancement of the data is central to Teilhard's understanding of the scientific process and of the transformation (transubstantiation?) of the universe that Teilhard sees in his "Mass."

I. A Training of the Eyes

For Teilhard and many other scientists, science is an ongoing process; it is alive. He believed faith should be the same. The vitality of the sciences is found in the scientific method, a method that involves assuming a hypothesis and then seeing if it works. Does it explain the data? If it does, the hypothesis is accepted; if it does not, one modifies it or sets it aside and looks for another hypothesis. But can or should the claims of Christian faith be considered a set of hypothetical truths subject to verification? Teilhard believed they should and argued that for the faith to regain its vigor it must be taken that way. Believers might look down on the hypothesis as a lesser knowledge than faith, but Teilhard did not. For him the hypothesis is "the supreme spiritual act by which the dust cloud of experience takes on form and is kindled at the fire of knowledge."[2] Today many believers would be reluctant to see their faith as a hypothesis. A hypothesis is conditional; it is to be tried out in experience and possibly rejected. Teilhard believed the faith should undergo a similar test; many of his Jesuit friends did not see it that way.

Teilhard had a close Jesuit friend, Auguste Valensin, who was a noted scholar and author of many learned books and articles. But at one point Teilhard observed that his friend Valensin was making a *cassette close* out of the articles of faith. Valensin had a strong faith, and accepted all that the Church taught, and then went about his academic work—studies in philosophy and world literature. But Teilhard objected, "If Christianity offers us nothing but certain *'cassettes closes,'* then we will soon throw both Christianity and the *cassettes* overboard."[3] And this is precisely what he saw happening. Christianity was seen as a packet of claims that you accepted or not; if you accepted the claims, you went about your work, as did Fr. Valensin. Many other people came to wonder why they bothered to hold on to the Catholic *cassette* at all, so they let it go.

Taking the faith as a hypothesis would involve bringing the *cassette* into the turmoil of life to see if it survives. Teilhard found it did. Consider how the hypothesis affects "the dust cloud of experience." Teilhard was a research scientist, and by his field-work helped reconfigure the geology of Asia; he also became much involved in the search for early human remains. Fellow scientists have told of his remarkable ability to spot a primitive stone tool amid the broken rocks of a gravel bed.[4] Most people would see the "tool" as only one more broken rock. What enabled Teilhard to see it differently was his practice in the field. Teilhard had worked with thousands of such stones and tried to understand the humans who fashioned them. He knew their tool-making techniques and had tried them himself. He knew that over time tool-making went through different phases as the skill in tool-making advanced: early stone age, middle stone age, and so forth. With much practice in the field, Teilhard's eyes could quickly spot a tool. In a rock pile, one rock would light up with meaning; implications would follow about those who had made and used it. Many eyes had seen the broken rock, but it could take on meaning only for someone familiar with the field and whose mind was working with several hypotheses concerning the development of tools in Asia. To the eyes of such a one the small scratches (differences) would stand out with great significance, and one's hypothesis (a union) concerning the history of tool-making in Asia would gain a nuance.

Seeing is more than what strikes the retina of the eye; yet all seeing begins that way. Teilhard would have it that when we first opened our eyes, we saw "light and things around us all jumbled up and all on a single plane."[5] Perhaps the first development in our ability to see was in seeing a three-dimensional world. Seeing three-dimensionally involves an *interpretation* of the jumble of colors that strike the two retinas. One might argue that the mind has added the interpretation to the data in order to render it coherent, still it results in the interpretation working its way back into the perception itself so that we *see* differently than before. We *see* a three-dimensional world. By further developing our vision we come to see in many additional ways. To illustrate with other examples: a person who *works* with car repair can open the hood of a disabled car and suddenly "see" the problem, while someone else would see only a jumble of dark metal and wires. A person who *works* on Wall Street can turn to the stock market pages and "see" a recession beginning, while another sees only columns of more or less meaningless numbers. Teilhard suggests Christians also need a training of the eyes to see as Christians (the car mechanic and the stock broker had to learn to *see* in their respective fields). Teilhard learned to see in his field of paleontology; but Teilhard also had learned to *see* in the field of Christology. For Teilhard the scientist, the stone tool would "light up" with meaning; for Teilhard the priest, the world would light up in a similar way. But note: the stone or the world itself would light with meaning only for one who works in the field, for one who has had a training of the eyes.

This "lighting up" can be explained by the phrase of Teilhard considered earlier: "union differentiates." In first introducing the phrase, Teilhard told of the unity of elements in a biological organism, but then he presented it as characteristic of a good hypothesis. If the hypothesis is true it will bring a unity to the data, and at the same time enable the data itself to acquire a sharpness of feature. In doing any kind of research (historical, literary, scientific) we come up with a hypothesis; then we see how the data looks in the light of the hypothesis. Perhaps all the data do not fit and the details seem blurred. So we might modify the hypothesis or check the data, but we begin to feel uneasy. The hypothesis has given a certain unity, but, if in gaining unity the data has been distorted, we suspect the hypothesis is faulty. Yet there are times when we come up with a hypothesis that breathes new life into the data; the details stand out more sharply than ever; this is unity differentiating the details. We judge the hypothesis to be correct if it makes the details stand forth. For example: we might claim Oswald acting alone shot John F. Kennedy. With that in mind we look to the data. Does it all seem to fit? Does our hypothesis make the data light up, stand forth with new meaning? Or does it distort some of the data or ignore it all together? For Teilhard, when we work with a true hypothesis, "The landscape lights up and yields its secrets."[6] This is what Teilhard could *see* in the broken rock; in considering it a tool, the small scratches and chips (the landscape) seemed to light up with meaning. But the landscape would do so only for one working in the field.

Early in his primary work, *The Phenomenon of Man*, Teilhard wrote a few paragraphs on nuclear physics. But before doing so he apologized for not having "that contact which comes from experiment and not from reading and makes all the difference."[7] The working scientist has a very different perspective than the well-read reader of science. And the difference can be seen by reconsidering the phrase: union differentiates.

Teilhard believed that differentiation of the data is what enables a scientist to tell whether a hypothesis is true. For example: in *The Phenomenon of Man* Teilhard argues that evolution has a direction and that direction is toward increased consciousness. That is his hypothesis; it claims that evolution is not simply the random process postulated by orthodox Darwinism; rather, it claims there is a generalized move in evolution toward greater consciousness. The evidence for this can be seen in the fossil record that shows the increasing development of the nervous system and the larger brain size found in many forms of life—in general, these are indications of increased consciousness. To defend his claim Teilhard argues that when the tree of life is considered in terms of elaborating more complex nervous systems, the whole picture of evolution clarifies. That is, if in holding the hypothesis that evolution has a direction and that the direction is toward the increase of consciousness, this "confers on the tree of life a sharpness of feature, an impetus, which is incontestably the hall-mark of truth. Such coherence...could not be the result of chance."[8] The "coherence" tells of the union, while the "sharpness of feature" tells of the differentiation of the data; the data mutually clarify themselves in light of the theory, union differentiates the data. Teilhard claims that to one familiar with the myriad details of evolution, the tree of life would stand forth with new meaning in light of his claim. To consider another example: Teilhard claimed that education is integral to evolution. Then to justify the claim he adds that the hypothesis "derives unquestionable verification from the very coherence which it brings to the whole landscape, and the relief into which it throws it."[9] Again, the coherence is the unity and the landscape brought into sharp relief is the differentiation of the data. Union differentiates.

A number of scientists, including Albert Einstein, Paul Dirac, and Werner Heisenberg, have spoken of the beauty of a scientific theory. Their texts make brief allusions to beauty without explanation. I would argue that Teilhard's "union differentiates" is the best way of understanding what they meant. In science beauty "occurs" when one sees an immensity of data coming together in the unity of a simple theory. A valid theory (or hypothesis) makes the data light up and cohere, while an invalid theory blurs, distorts, or omits some of the data it should unify. Thus, beauty can be seen as the unity differentiating the data.

Back to the difference between reading science and working in science: if one has not done fieldwork in evolution, or toolmaking, or auto mechanics, one would not see the world light up. Consider an example. From our reading we probably know the famous formula of Einstein, $E = mc^2$. But not many people work in that field. Yes, most educated people know that E stands for energy, and m for mass, and c for the speed of light. Most people stop there and accept the claim on faith without further thought, for we have nothing further to think about. If we do not work in a field related to the physics of relativity, it is a *cassette close*. We accept it on faith because we know that is what the scientific community holds, but it has no effect on our experience. We do not see our world differently after hearing it. We do not find experiential details standing forth more sharply, nor does our world light up. One theory is no more "beautiful" than another, for beauty occurs when a theory lights up the details. If tomorrow we heard that scientists had found Einstein was wrong and that with correction his theory should have read $E = mc^3$, we would dutifully replace the old *cassette* with a new one. It would be another revelation of sorts from higher authorities, but it would not enable us to see a different world. Since we do not work in the field, the change would add no unity (coherence) to our vision and it would not sharpen the details of our world. Some people take the Bible that way, as a *cassette close*. They accept the Bible on the authority of God, or on the authority of a community they trust. They may memorize and recite its passages, but the Bible does not light up their world; it does not give coherence to their lives. They accept it dutifully, much like they accept $E = mc^2$. It is a higher truth revealed to them. Then Christian faith or Catholic faith would consist in affirming the correct creed, while (too bad for them!) non-Christians have been handed the wrong *cassette*. Then the issue for the thoughtful Christian becomes: Do the claims of the Christian creed affect the world one sees? Do they light up the landscape of one's life? Do they give beauty to what had been the drab details of what we do? What would we see if we made Christian claims into working hypotheses?

II. Vision and the Hypothesis

Teilhard would speak of two kinds of knowledge. One is an abstract knowledge that is found in geometry and theology; it concerns the world of ideas and principles; for this type of knowledge he felt an instinctive distrust. But he told of a second type of knowledge that he favored; this concerned physics and mysticism. The difference between geometry, on the one hand, and physics, on the other, can help clarify the difference between the theology of principles that Teilhard did not trust and the mysticism that he did.[10] Both geometry and theology can form *cassettes closes;* they are complete structures—hopefully consistent. But physics is not. One can build the principles of geometry into elaborate systems; one can do the same with the principles of revealed theology. This was done with a certain brilliance during the Middle Ages. Today we do not believe things are so simple. For we know there are many different geometries (not only Euclidean) and know there are many different theologies (not only Christian). If each is consistent in itself, there would seem to be no way to prefer one *cassette* to another. Each is what Teilhard would see as a pseudo-absolute.

If this were the whole story, the sensible solution would be to mistrust them all and get on with one's life.

But physicists have found a way out of such dilemmas. They test geometries in experience. The time has come to test theologies in a similar way. For centuries the Euclidean geometry worked wonders, but the time came when the universe began giving the physicists data that would not fit the Euclidean system. So the physicists adopted another geometry that made the data cohere. The new geometry lit up the details they recently had been finding. So they accepted the alternate geometry. Such is the living reality of modern physics. It is an ongoing process.

The geometry of Euclid tells of a world of perfect form that can be understood as an alternate world; but also in the history of Western science it has enabled us to better understand the present world. Consider one such moment: Archimedes knew his geometry, plane and solid, but he was also a physicist. Archimedes took the heavenly truths of Euclid and applied them on earth. Stories tell of Archimedes wanting to know if the king's crown was made of solid gold. While considering the issue, he stepped into his bath water only to see the water rise. He shouted, "Eureka, I have found it." His excitement was in seeing the solid geometry of Euclid in the rising water. I believe that Teilhard, during his wartime years, did much the same: he took the heavenly truths of Christianity out of the sky and shouted with excitement. (A sense of excitement runs through all his wartime writings.) The dust of experience, the experiences of war with its monotony and horror, were kindled into fire. (His wartime essays convey a passion that sometimes obscures what he is saying; yet one can suspect this excitement is responsible for much of his extraordinary appeal.) He tells of the gospel as lived experience. He was caught in a war that was brutal and ugly, yet by seeing it in gospel terms he found the horrors of war light up with meaning. The wartime essays are often complex and difficult, but in them Teilhard is saying, "Eureka," with an excitement that is contagious. His theology had become his experience. His theology was no longer a *cassette close;* it was *seen* in the world of experience. As Archimedes did with the geometry of Euclid, Teilhard is asking us to do with Christian theology: make it a working hypothesis. He claims that Christian theology will give coherence (union) to our experience and sharpen (differentiate) the details of our life and our work.

To illustrate what Christian theology can do to experience, consider a phrase from the New Testament that was an important faith-claim for Teilhard during his wartime years: "To the one who believes all things work together unto good." It is a slightly adapted phrase from St. Paul's letter to the Romans (8:28): "In everything God works for good to those who love him." Teilhard took the line to experience, and one of his wartime essays, "Operative Faith," tells of working with the phrase. With the hypothesis that God was bringing good out of the war he could conclude that "the elements cohere in a rigorously differentiated individual nature," and "everything remains the same as far as phenomena are concerned, but at the same time everything becomes luminous, animated, instinct with love."[11] By holding the hypothesis of Christian faith the landscape of war lit up with meaning. But the essay ends with a warning: if one claims to understand what he is saying here without putting one's hand to the plow, that person is deluding herself or himself. The plow is the world of experience; there our work must be guided by the hypotheses of Christian faith. We must test our beliefs in experience. Otherwise we can study the texts of the New Testament or the texts of Teilhard until we know them well. Then we can add, "The Theology of the New Testament," or "The Theology of Teilhard" to our set of theological *cassettes*. They have become theologies we can explain, not a mysticism we can live. And our world has not lit up.

Teilhard also modified the revelation. He changed the phrase, "To the one who believes all things work together unto good" to "all things work together unto Christ." This Christ is the ultimate Christ, the one of whom St. Paul's letter to the Colossians said, "In him all things hold together." It is the risen Christ, Christ-Omega, the one into whom the universe is being drawn, the "cosmic Christ." Teilhard spoke of seeing Christ, but it was not simply the Christ of whom he had read; it is Christ visible. "Like other real objects, Christ is 'experienced.'"[12] He is "experienced" as Archimedes experienced the geometry of Euclid.

Teilhard asks us, "What prevents you from taking Christ into your arms, only your inability to see." For Teilhard, there is no phrase of Christian theology quite as important as the phrase from the Mass: "This is my Body." It is the God-man claiming the world as his body. If one believes the claim, one's world is illuminated. This can be seen in a prayer found late in his "Mass."

> Glorious Lord Christ: the divine influence secretly diffused and active in the depths of matter, and the dazzling center where all the innumerable fibers of the multiple meet....you whose forehead is of the whiteness of snow, whose eyes are of fire, and whose feet are brighter than molten gold; you whose hands imprison the stars; you who are the first and the last, the living and the dead and the risen again...it is to you to whom my being cried out with a desire as vast as the universe, "In truth, you are my Lord and my God."[13]

"My Lord and my God!" It is what St. Thomas said when he touched the risen Lord. Teilhard used the same phrase, for like St. Thomas he found that Christ had become visible/tangible. He was able to see as well as to believe. It is the prayer one can make only after one has taken Gospel passages as working hypotheses. By doing so Teilhard found the world itself took on a radiant meaning and all the details of the human landscape came to life. That is what he claims we will see if we take the Gospel as guiding hypotheses.

Teilhard wanted us to see the risen Christ, so he presented many of his works as attempts to see and help others see.[14] Many people in today's world have a radically pessimistic view of their own future and the future of the world. They see aging and entropy, death and darkness, as their future and it colors all they see; and it all goes back to the hypothesis by which they live. Consider again how what we know affects what we see: suppose scientists would announce a large comet is heading toward the earth and it will strike our planet in three days, ending all life. Even before the comet strikes, the world itself would appear radically altered: it would *appear* doomed. In the words of Teilhard, we would see how "the paralyzing poison of death eats irresistibly into everything we make—and everything we do."[15] But if we believe that all things will find their consummation in Christ, the world itself will appear different (the poison of death will have "vanished from the heart of all things"): things would light up with possibilities, for all will be made new. Some such change of perspective frequently happens at a moment of conversion: people suddenly see their own lives differently. They see that Christ was present throughout what seemed long and fruitless struggles; everything seems to make sense; all their confused gropings gain a unity and details stand out with a new sharpness.

Teilhard asks, "What prevents you from enfolding Christ in your arms? Only your inability to see."[16] He has many statements that speak of seeing/touching Christ that are surprisingly immediate: God is "perceived by our eyes," "One feels in things the touch of Christ's hand," "Like other real objects Christ is experienced," "the world...takes on Christ in its inner substance," we have a "perception of the divine spread everywhere." The divine presence unifies and exalts "all that is most specific." God "pushes to its furthest possible limit the differentiation among the creatures he concentrates in himself."[17] When looking at the rocks, Teilhard had developed his eyes to the point he could "see" a tool where others saw only a broken rock; likewise he had developed his eyes so that he could "see" Christ present where others saw only the horrors of war. Teilhard's hypothesis had taken the dust of war and brought it together into the fire of an understanding. Teilhard writes, "The man who *dares* to believe reaches a sphere of created reality in which things, while retaining their habitual texture, seem to be made out of a different substance....Through the operation of faith, Christ appears."[18] Things seem "to be made out of a different substance." This apparent change of substance would resemble the "transubstantiation" that occurs in the Mass. For in the process, Christ will "become the most substantial Reality that exists"[19] On several occasions he would speak of faith changing the world and quote a Latin phrase from the epistle to the Hebrews: *Fides substantia rerum* (Faith is the substance of things [Heb 11:1]).[20] Our faith gives the insubstantial world its substance. For in us it is rendered eternal.

III. How the World Changes in the Mass

In Teilhard's "Mass," we begin by gathering into our souls all that constitutes our world. And all of us live a world that is coming to life and a world that is dying. We feel our own aspirations and disappointments, but we also feel the aspirations and disappointments of those we know and care for. In the offertory this world is seen to be reaching for a common soul, much as the scientist finds the data he or she has gathered seem to be reaching for a unified understanding (even if one is not directly thinking of the matter, the data in our mind seem to arrange and rearrange themselves in attempts at coming together). Then in the consecration, God, speaking through the priest, claims the growth of the world as his body and then claims the disappointments as his blood; and, if we can see the world that way, our world, in its weal and in its woe, lights up with meaning. Following the consecration of his "Mass," Teilhard writes: "The flame has lit up the whole world from within."[21] A very similar transformation takes place when the scientist, gathering in his mind an abundance of data (as the priest gathers his experience in the offertory), considers the data in the light of a hypothesis (as does the priest in saying the words of consecration over his world). If the hypothesis makes the scientific data light up with clarity and meaning, the scientist considers the hypothesis to be true. This is what Teilhard, as scientist, did in claiming the tree of life shows organisms moving toward a greater cerebralization and consciousness. It is also what he did as a priest when he claimed the advance of life was forming the body of Christ. In regarding the data from these perspectives, all the elements take on "a sharpness of feature, an impetus, which is incontestably the hall-mark of truth." The hypothesis effects "a significant transformation" in how we see.[22] One could say the elements seem lit from within or they seem animated by a common soul. They seem more deeply themselves as they are united in a hypothesis: union differentiates. Teilhard sees something very similar in the consecration of his "Mass": there we see the growth of the world as Christ's body and its pain as his blood; as above, this too is "a significant transformation" in how we see. This is the *vision* that follows the consecration, but the Mass does not stop with vision.

Teilhard offers his Mass in the morning and foresees the day ahead. He has had his vision of the world changed by the words of consecration. Now he must act on what he sees. For Teilhard, this is the communion. He must pass from vision to action; throughout the coming day he must live a consecrated world. Can he accept the "fiery bread" set before him (the opportunities for growth that are often difficult) as a communion with the body of Christ? But more difficult to accept are the diminishments. Can he accept the chalice (the disappointments setbacks, and even his death) as a communion with the blood of Christ? If he can accept them that way, that is what they are. And he will come to know both the growth and setbacks of his life as only the gently alternating phases of a single communion.

In Teilhard's retreat notes from 1906 and 1907—long before he wrote his "Mass on the World"—he was seeing all he did as a "Perpetual Communion."[23] Communion then became a key word in his first essay ("Cosmic Life"). While writing his "Mass" he told of a pan-communion by which he was "obsessed and intoxicated."[24] For throughout his writings, he speaks of communion in many contexts. But the Mass involves more than communion. It was only later with his scientific training that he was able to complete his understanding of the Mass with an offertory and a consecration; he had to become aware of how the scientific hypothesis gave him a new way of seeing the world. Under the hypothesis that God was claiming the world as his body, he found the events of his life taking on a surprising intensity. He felt that by the hypothesis his world had lit up. The hypothesis had vindicated itself and it was up to him to live each event as Christ building his body or shedding his blood.

Teilhard would come to speak of the scientist as a priest.[25] For both scientist and priest are involved in a similar process; they are transforming a world by what they believe about it. They are both standing before a world that is coming to be, and over it they both invoke phrases that light up their respective worlds from within. This change of the world one "sees" became central to Teilhard's understanding of the consecration when he wrote his "Mass on the World."

Teilhard would teach us to see with the eyes of faith. That is the training he would offer for our eyes. For there are times we live our faith like Teilhard's Jesuit friend, Auguste Valensin; it is a *cassette close* that we duly affirm. We affirm it as readers, not as scientists, not with our hand to the plow. We can find life is only a dust of incoherent experiences. We ignore our own life and turn to a mysticism of unknowing while life becomes a dull stupor; occasionally we endure great events, but we do not recognize them and lack words adequate to speak of them. Teilhard tells us that by making Gospel phrases his working hypotheses he found all things lighting up from within. So like Archimedes ("Eureka"), he would speak with excitement and wonder at what he had seen. It was not the geometry of Euclid seen in the bath water, but the Lord Christ seen in wartime events. Can the Christian hypotheses bring coherence to the data of our life? Or to the dust of our death? Teilhard claimed they could. Geometricians, theologians, and others whose faith is guarded in closed cassettes will not understand this, but physicists and mystics will. For their hand is on the plow.

Notes

1. C, 74.
2. A, 9; V, 205.
3. Li, 363.
4. Barbour, 35; Cuenot, 156.
5. P, 216.
6. P, 32.
7. P, 39.
8. P, 146.

9. F, 32.
10. Li, 269.
11. W, 240, 244, 246.
12. W, 246.
13. HM, 131, 132.
14. W, 15; P, 31; D, 46.
15. A, 400.
16. D, 46.
17. D, 116.
18. W, 246.
19. W, 246.
20. D, 137; W, 226, 239n.
21. HM, 123.
22. P, 146.
23. Nr, 124.
24. HM, 48.
25. LMF, 149.

3.

THE SCIENTIFIC WORK
OF TEILHARD WHILE WRITING
"THE MASS ON THE WORLD"

*"Even at the peak of my spiritual trajectory I was never to
feel at home unless immersed in an Ocean of Matter."*

Teilhard was working at the Paris Museum when a Jesuit
from the Province of Lille, Emile Licent, began sending the
museum fossils he had found in China. Boule turned them over to
Teilhard and Teilhard began a correspondence with Licent. Like
Teilhard, Licent had been enthusiastic about natural history since
he was a boy; then as a young Jesuit he began planning a center of
scientific and Christian studies that he would set up in China.
Some have described him as brusk and dictatorial, but he was also
regarded as an honest, hard-working man who adapted well to living in China: he learned Chinese (Teilhard never did) and dealt
effectively with workers, warlords, and wandering bandits. Licent
went to China in 1914 with a doctorate in science (entomology),
determined to be a geographer, geologist, naturalist, and ethnog-
rapher. He was by nature a collector and set up a three-storey
museum in Tientsin. In the summer of 1922, following advice
given him by Belgian missionaries, he went to the Ordos Desert,
where he found a fair number of early human tools. The Ordos is
bordered on the South by the Great Wall of China and on the
other three sides by the Yellow River (it is within the "Great
Bend" of the Yellow). From west to east it is about 300 to 400 kilometers across and has deep layers of mostly yellow loess (wind-

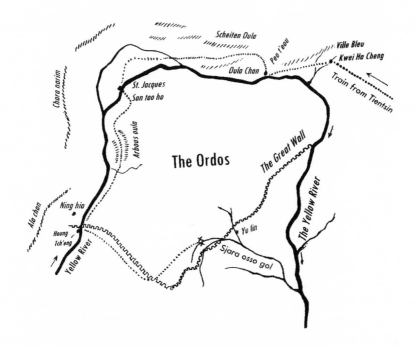

Map of the Ordos showing
Teilhard's round-about journey to the Sjara Osso Gol

blown dust that has hardened) on a base of hardened sandstone from the age of dinosaurs.

Here in 1922, Licent found some primitive stone tools in the walls of the canyon cut into the Ordos by the Sjara Osso Gol (Mongolian for Yellow Waters, a tributary of the Yellow River). He sent several tools and other materials to the Paris Museum for study; they were the first traces of early humans ever found in China. In the same area Licent told of finding a fossilized human femur and a small piece of bone with human markings on it; because they were not found in situ, this greatly diminished their importance. Licent planned to return there the following summer and invited Teilhard to join him in the exploration. Teilhard, with the approval of his Jesuit superiors, decided to go. *The Museum national d'Histoire naturelle and the Ministere de l'Instruction publique* would sponsor the expedition, and in return for the better fossils, the museum would finance the expedition.

As Teilhard prepared to depart, Licent telegraphed him telling him of increased danger from bandits and suggested they not go. Not heeding the warning, Teilhard left from Marseilles on April 6 and arrived in Tientsin on May 23. First he looked briefly through the materials Licent had collected in his museum, the most significant of which were additional tools and other objects found in the summer of 1922. Because of bandits, drought, and the plague, they decided to approach their goal in the Ordos by a roundabout route. "The Chinese authorities agreed to give us passports while declaring they washed their hands of what might happen to us."[1] So on either the 11th or 12th of June, Teilhard and Licent took a train from Tientsin to the end of the rail line at Pao Teou. There Licent hired workers, bought pack animals, and made arrangements for travel. They set out with two mules, three donkeys, five muleteers, two servants, and a military escort.[1] Because of bandits and a drought, their indirect route involved their going west-northwest without crossing the Yellow River. This gave them an opportunity to study two mountain ridges, the Oula Chan and the Scheiten Oula. These were found to be formed of layers of pre-Cambrian rocks that were folded down into the crystalline strata at an angle of about 80 degrees. Passing across these ridges, they followed the Yellow River west and then south to a French mission station, St. Jacques at San Tao Ho, where Teilhard told of seeing the mass of red clay that was from the Miocene (7-2.6 million years old) beneath the gray loess of the Quaternary (the last million years). The expedition crossed the Yellow River and entered the Ordos proper. Here they found on the ground (not in situ) a scratcher and some dubious tools of red quartzite.

Traveling between two additional ridges, the Arbous Ulla and the Yinze Chan, they found these ridges formed anticlines steepening eastward, and the carboniferous rocks here contained some marine intercalations. The explorers continued south, crossing the Great Wall, and on July 22, as they walked eastward parallel to the Great Wall 25 kilometers east of Houng Tch'eng, they found the first ancient hearth (campsite) found in China, "a typical paleolithic hearth in perfectly stratified deposits." This was 12 meters down in the loess in a bluff that was 25 meters high. Around the hearth were hundreds of broken and worked stones. They collected an immense quantity of them. The tools were points and scrapers made of quartzites, phasamites, and silified limestone. Teilhard saw them as comparable with the Mousterian tools (a flake-based industry associated with the Neanderthals in Europe) or early Aurignacian tools (started about 40,000 years ago associated with the Cro Magnons of Europe). But there were also small flints that showed a finer workmanship. "In any place where the loess has weathered out, worked Paleolithic stones can be found, lying on the ground." Mixed with these worked stones were burned and broken bones (the bones had been split to get at the marrow). These were mostly from wild asses, but there were also bones from hyenas, antelope, and bison; the shells of ostrich eggs suggested that their contents had been eaten. Recent studies of the material indicate that "Ordos Man" lived about 35,000 years ago. Within one kilometer of the area they found four other hearths that were smaller than the first. As the first ancient hearths found in Asia, they were of major importance.

Teilhard and Licent continued eastward south of the Great Wall and then crossed it to enter the Ordos again and arrive at the Sjara Oso Gol (their original goal) in the first days of August. "I don't regret our six weeks' wandering on mule-back across mountains and deserts....we came across important—and unexpected—geological and paleontological finds, which are probably worth more than all the bones of rhinoceroses, horses, and various animals that we are now engaged in extracting from the cliffs of the Shara-Uso-Gol."[3] On the canyon walls north of Siao K'iao Pan in the lower part of a Quaternary formation they found paleolithic worked stones about 70 meters below the Ordos plain. These were on the sides of what Teilhard called "a curious little stream"—the Sjara Oso Gol, a river/stream that was only about 1,000 years old, but already had cut a canyon 70 and 80 meters into the soft loess, leaving coves in the canyon walls where abundant fossils could be found. Some canyons were 200 meters deep.[4]

Mongols were living in caves along the sides of the river. Here the expedition spent much of their time in tents, and in a letter Teilhard speaks of their living on steppes ("The Mass on the World" speaks of the steppes of Asia); it was probably written in this area. They explored along the canyons here for twenty four days—their longest stay in one place. Here they employed about twenty workers, about half Chinese and half Mongol. They found many worked stones and an amazing quantity of broken animal bones on a bed of hard, blue clay. The paleoliths of this area are amazingly small, probably because no larger stones were to be found in the area. Here chipped tools were common while true tools were rare. Though most were small, one scratcher measures 5 x 7 centimeters. Most of the tools are made of hard, black quartzite. The many animal bones, probably the remains of a kitchen midden, were highly fossilized and came from thirty three species of mammals and eleven species of birds. They also found an abundance of antlers (three hundred from gazelles) broken intentionally to be used as handles for tools. As for human remains, they found two thigh bones and one bone from an upper arm, but again these were not found in situ. This was a great disappointment, as the primary object of their work was to find human bones or teeth. (In 1978–80, the Chinese Academy of Science mounted a large expedition that went to the same site and found nineteen fossilized bones or partial bones of Ordos Man.[5]) After twenty-four days working there, Teilhard wrote, "I think I will miss the calm and picturesque campsite of the Chara-O-Gol [sic], where one can live in great freedom wearing nothing but a Chinese blouse"[6]

Teilhard and Licent crossed again to the south of the Great Wall and came to You Fang T'eou, where they found a third site about 90 kilometers south of where they had just been digging. Here tools were rare; only six were found. The tools were small and found about 160 meters beneath the top of the loess. The tools seemed more primitive than at the other two sites. In 1920 Licent had found similar tools at another site about 80 kilometers farther south, but they did not go there. On September 9, Teilhard wrote, "We will try to leave here in four days with more than 30 boxes for Ning Hia, where we will embark on the Huang Ho [Yellow River]. But on the way we would like to dig at the hearth."[7] This referred to the hearth they had found earlier; in returning there they found additional tools, but nothing of great note. Soon Teilhard is writing to a friend of his plans to "make our way into the deepest clefts in the mountain where the Red Earth stands out like wounded flesh under the thick layers of grey." The image of the earth as flesh is a significant theme in "The Mass on the World." In the area around that first hearth, the loess rested on red earth; there was further red earth on the right bank of the Yellow River as they headed back. At Ning Hia they loaded their materials on a large raft and floated with the current down to Pao Teou, where they with their crates of materials boarded the train for Tientsin.

On returning to Tientsin, Teilhard studied the fossils they had collected and decided it was worth staying in China another year to continue his search for ancient human bones. He wrote to Marcellin Boule for additional support and to the rector of the Institut Catholique where he had been teaching and asked to stay through the summer of 1924. Boule agreed that it was worth waiting to make a return expedition, and, impressed by all he sent back, arranged for the museum to sponsor them for a second year. The rector of the Institut extended Teilhard's leave of absence. Teilhard and Licent had hopes of returning to the Ordos the following summer but, probably because of increasing reports of bandits, they explored a different area to the northeast. Here their findings were less significant. He, together with Licent, would publish several accounts of their findings. The first two were "On the Geology of the Northern, Western and Southern Borders of the Ordos" and "On the Discovery of a Paleolithic Industry in Northern China"; these appeared in the *Bulletin of the Geological Society of China*, volume II, 1924. These and several other articles concerning the 1923 exploration can be found in volumes II and III of *l'Oeuvre scientifique* of Teilhard. See especially "*Observations geologiques sur la bordure occidentale et meridionale de l'Ordos,*" a report Teilhard and Licent gave in Peking in February 1924, and "*Observations complementaires sur la Geologie de l'Ordos,*" which includes numerous pictures. A thorough account is found in *Le Paleolithique de la Chine*, volume III, July 1928.

In 1934 J. Gunnar Anderson wrote an account of all the work in geology and paleontology that had been done in China until that time. One chapter is devoted to the work of Licent and Teilhard. He ends the chapter by saying, "The discovery by the two French scientists of Paleolithic man in the Ordos desert was in every respect an exemplary and particularly brilliant scientific achievement....The triumph of this epoch-making discovery can with equal justice be attributed to Licent's enthusiasm and initiative and to Teilhard's perfected and exact scientific method."[8]

Notes

1. T enC, 55.
2. Barbour, 26-27.
3. LLZ, 51-52.
4. T enC, 71.
5. Jia, 22.
6. T enC, 69.
7. UL, Breuil, Sept. 9, 1923.
8. Andersson, 155.

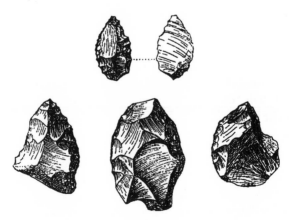

Stone implements from Sjara Osso Gol

4.

THE MASS AND THE SALVATION
OF THE WORLD

*"The Eucharistic Consecration has a natural meaning
which extends to the whole of Cosmogenesis."*

*(Some passages of the text that follows might be difficult, yet if one
continues reading, the difficulties will become clear and one will better
appreciate both new depths in Teilhard and in the Mass itself.)*

Many religious people consider love for the world a vanity and
an obstacle to their religious life, for the world and all that is in it will
perish. Recently this ancient religious teaching received support
from modern physics, which claims that the universe is moving
toward death, disintegration, and chaos, a move termed *entropy*.
Entropy tells of structures breaking down whenever energy comes
into play, so that eventually (after billions of years) the universe will
sink into dissolution. Teilhard was aware of both the religious tradition and the scientific claim, yet he continued to speak of the "salvation and success of the universe itself." In additional phrases he told
of the "fulfillment of this world," of "some crowning glory for the
universe"; it will "end in ecstasy" in God.[1] The universe will attain
its fulfillment through the Mass, "an action that changes the world."
And "each communion, each consecration…is a notch further in the
incorporation of the Cosmos into Christ."[2] "The Eucharistic consecration has a natural meaning which extends to the whole of
Cosmogenesis."[3] To explain how the Mass transforms the world, one
must consider the whole of the philosophy of Teilhard.

For Teilhard the salvation of the world is achieved in two
steps. The first step is natural: "Everything in the Cosmos is for

Spirit." The second step is supernatural: "Everything, in Spirit, is for Christ."[4] Spirit is a translation of the French *esprit*. But *esprit* can be translated into English as either spirit or mind. In general, but not always, the present text will favor translating *esprit* as mind. That would give the two steps: "Everything in the cosmos is for mind, and everything in mind is for Christ." (Teilhard's *esprit* refers to the human mind/spirit and only rarely to *le Saint Esprit*.)

I. A *Reversal of Direction*

Teilhard wrote the first of the essays that would make him famous when he was thirty five years old and serving in the French army during World War I. He called it "Cosmic Life" to affirm that the cosmos itself is alive. Early in the essay he recalls several moments when the universe seemed to summon him. On one such occasion he was gazing over a dreary expanse of desert and heard the call, on another he was watching the waves of the ocean, and on a third occasion he felt called to lose himself in the shadows of a deep forest. At all such moments he felt possessed by a yearning to let go of the anxieties and toil of life, relax, and sink back into the world that had cradled him: "Matter was calling me." The earth itself appeared as the "indestructible essence from which all emerges and into which all returns, the starting point of all growth and the limit of all disintegration."[5] So he allowed himself to drift into matter, believing his "over-tense activity might indefinitely become ever more relaxed." As he released his hold of himself he more or less dissolved into a bliss-giving repose. He had decided to merge with the great All, thinking, "If I was to be All, I must be fused with all."[6] His conscious mind was slipping into what Sigmund Freud would call "oceanic feelings."

But as Teilhard drifted downward he suddenly stopped: "It was then that faith in life saved me." Without explanation he reversed direction, made a "complete turnabout," and announced, "We must travel with our backs turned to matter and not try to return to it and be absorbed into it."[7] His effort to relax and dissolve was "hopelessly mistaken," he had gone "completely astray." After his reversal he would identify with the tense and rising current of life, the current known as evolution. Evolution is seen as a movement away from dissolution and into ever more complex structures; it is a movement to consciousness and freedom, to "absolute fuller being." These two movements, one that would relax into dissolution and nothingness and the other that would struggle toward greater complexity and being, underlie all of Teilhard's thought. He would connect the first with entropy and the second with evolution, and his writings would abundantly contrast the two currents.[8] The two movements would lead to very different goals: entropy would lead to a *materialist* pantheism (god identified with matter), while evolution would lead to a spiritual pantheism (God as the Soul unifying all things). He would see this spiritual pantheism to be consonant with Christianity and spoke of a "Christian pantheism," for St. Paul had spoken of a future when God would be "All in all."[9]

Pantheism (All God-ism) is a term that has not been acceptable in the Christian tradition, but recently many Christian theologians have used a somewhat similar term, pan*en*theism (All *in* God-ism). It seems Teilhard would have used this term if he knew of it and it were available to him. Lacking it he spoke of a Christian pantheism, a Christian face of pantheism, a second species of pantheism, a pantheism of form, or other terms suggesting a modified pantheism. But, for Teilhard, "Every religion worthy of the name is pantheist."[10]

When Teilhard relaxed and partially surrendered to matter it was in order to become one with matter, the great All *(le Tout)*. It had seemed that efforts at maintaining a personal identity separated him from the rest of nature, so to identify with the All he would renounce his individual identity. In doing so he believed being was to be found in the ultimate "Matter of matters"—the All with which he sought to identify. But after making his reversal he claimed that unity and being were not to be found in matter at all, but only in the opposite direction, in a "higher Centre common to all developments, the Form of forms."[11] Teilhard's reversal can be seen as a switch from a unity in matter to a unity of form.

Teilhard had been trained in the scholastic tradition in philosophy in which the form of a living being was called its soul. So

61

Teilhard would speak of this "higher Centre," the "Form of forms," as the "World Soul"—a term found in Stoic philosophy. Following his reversal he would no longer seek a unity in matter (in fact, he would insist that matter lacks all unity), but in the single Soul of the World. For it is the soul of an organism that unites the bodily elements (accordingly, when the soul leaves the body in death, the body disintegrates).

Teilhard used passages from St. Paul to see the World Soul as the risen Christ, the one who unites the elements of the world: "In him all things hold together" (Col 1:17); thus, we constitute his body and he is our higher Soul. It would be in terms of such a Soul that St. Paul says, "It is no longer I who live, but Christ lives in me" (Gal 2:20). That is, beyond his individual soul St. Paul knew a higher Soul, the Christ. During World War I, Teilhard wrote an essay titled, "The Soul of the World."[12] He began by telling of an increasing number of people letting go of their Christian faith because Christ was presented to them in such a way that no longer met their aspirations; they wanted to hope and love in a more complete way than Christianity seemed to offer. They had become obscurely aware of a great Presence all about them, a "magnetic force" and a "never failing spring within," an awareness that inspired poets and nourished the mystics—while the Church presented images of Christ only as a particular individual, a detached fragment that set people in opposition to one another. To meet the aspirations of today's humanity, Teilhard proposed a pantheist form of Christianity and, citing evidence in William James' *Varieties of Religious Experience*, argued that such a mysticism is no stranger to the Christian tradition. But, though pantheist images are found in St. Paul and the Christian mystics, Teilhard believed the Church's image of Christ did not measure up to human aspirations. Thus, many people were looking away from Christianity to find what would match their experience. To speak to these people, Teilhard proposed the cosmic Christ, that is, Christ as Soul of the World.

In telling of the world having a single Soul, Teilhard certainly recognized much disunity in the world—he wrote essays telling of the Soul of the World in the midst of a World War—but he believed the present disunity indicated that the body of Christ is only partially achieved. He would look back to see the long, slow work of evolution as a process constructing ever wider and more complex unities. We humans are the most complex unities it has produced, but evolution is not complete with us. Rather, we are to assist in the work of evolution by working toward the unity that will one day embrace all humanity; then the body of Christ will be complete—this will be the pleroma (the "completion," or the "fullness") spoken of by St. Paul. Since St. Paul says Christ's body "upbuilds itself in love" (Eph 4:16), Teilhard saw the central human task as working to develop a loving and unified world. But to achieve that loving unity, Christ's body needs a physical infrastructure involving science, education, politics, industry, and so forth. Thus, many forms of human work play a part in giving Christ a suitable body, a body in which he might attain his fullness (the pleroma), and then God will be "all in all" (Eph 1:23; 1 Cor 15:28; Col 3:14). Such is the pantheist or panentheist image of Christ Teilhard found in the writings of St. Paul and what he believed the Church should offer to people of the present age. At times he would refer to the final Christ as Omega, the last letter of the Greek alphabet. In the New Testament Christ calls himself the Alpha and the Omega (Rev 1:8, 21:6, 22:13), the beginning and the end.

Teilhard's reversal from matter to form occurred while he was studying theology in England before the war. But for several years he had difficulty understanding how humans could unite in a common Soul, for each individual seemed to constitute a radically independent unit. But during the war, he saw thousands of individuals acting with a common purpose and he came to believe all humanity might likewise join in a common action. While in the war he directly experienced such a unity: Teilhard so identified with his fellow troops that he sensed they shared a common soul. He wrote with amazement of the troops feeling drawn above themselves "by the force of a collective passion, we have a sense of rising to a higher level of human existence."[13] In this he could tell of being directly aware of "a Soul greater than my own," "the Soul of the Front."[14] It was not so much theory as an immediate experience, so he would claim, "Christ is already revealing himself, in the depths of men's hearts, as the Shepherd (the Animator) of the Universe."[15] He associated this claim with that of St. Paul, "It is no longer I who live, but Christ who lives in me" (Gal 2:20). Having shared in a common Soul, Teilhard could appreciate St. Paul's claim that we are to form one body, the body of Christ, an organism of sorts that builds itself up with love (Col 3:14).

When Teilhard first responded to the call of the universe, he sought a *fusion* with all things, but after making his reversal he spoke instead of a *communion* with all things (*com*munion suggests some individuality remains). His first essay ended by telling of a communion with the earth leading to a communion with God—and the word *communion* already suggests the Eucharist. To say how a communion would differ from a fusion, Teilhard developed the phrase "union differentiates." That is, there is a type of union in which the elements maintain their own character and even deepen their character as they unite with one another. This is the union exemplified in an organism where all the elements are united by a common life or soul while retaining their own individual character. So it is that we unite in the body of Christ and in the process become more deeply ourselves. In an organism the elements do not dissolve (fuse) into a blob (an undifferentiated mass); rather, their differences are heightened: "union differentiates." This organic unity is found in human love: the more lovers are able to unite, the more deeply they become themselves. They feel they share a common soul while believing they have finally become who they were meant to be. Teilhard quotes Blondel: "Love supposes a perfect distinction in a perfect union."[16]

When Teilhard wrote "Cosmic Life," he spoke of the move to fusion and relaxation as a move to Nirvana. At the time he had a very limited knowledge of Eastern religions. Later he gained a greater familiarity with them, yet he more or less retained his original understanding. He would sometimes call evolution and progress the Way of the West, and the way of entropy and fusion the Way of the East. He thought of these as two fundamental forms of mysticism. Mysticism involves a desire to enter an all-embracing unity; this unity can be either a unity of fusion or the organic unity found in sharing a common soul. By his reversal, Teilhard turned from the first toward the second. To understand Teilhard's judgment of the East consider the final words of the Buddha, "All compound things dissolve; work out your salvation with fear and trembling." In feeling the summons of the universe and first responding to it, Teilhard had moved toward letting his complex identity dissolve according to the Way of the East. By his reversal he adopted the Way of the West.

Just as Teilhard often set entropy and evolution in contrast, he often set their psychological equivalents—the Way of the East and the Way of the West—in contrast.[17] Today some people in the West have taken the Eastern approach and identify themselves as neo-Buddhists; to them the ultimate reality is to be found by dissolving into the great All. And some scientists, in looking for the ultimate particle, believe the absolute is found when things are reduced to their simplest material elements. Philosophers of science who would explain everything in terms of ultimate particles are known as reductionists. And accounts of entropy would seem to give them some support, for entropy tells of an eventual breakdown in all structures. Now that we are aware of entropy, is there any point in evolution? Buddhists have advised, "All worldly things perish, so accept the inevitable and dissolve," while Christians often advised, "All worldly things perish, so accept the inevitable and renounce the world for heaven." In either case there would be no salvation for the world. Yet for Teilhard the world will be saved—but only through humanity.

II. Teilhard as Individualist and Idealist

There are two elements in the thought of Teilhard that many familiar with his writings do not recognize. The first is his individualism. He claims "each one of us has, in reality, *his own* universe; he is its centre and he is called upon to introduce harmony into it."[18] He told a friend, "I've become so accustomed to living in 'my own universe,'"[19] and two of his essays are titled "My Universe." He assumed others did the same: "Every man forms a little world on his own."[20] He would sometimes speak of people as "monads," a philosophic term that suggests radically self-contained units. "Each monad, in turn, is to some degree the centre of the entire Cosmos."[21] "Another Man is, for each of us, another World, a rival World to our own, that is to the one centered around us."[22] In seeing troops moving into battle he saw them as "so many worlds" in conflict.[23] He urged that if we could *per impossibile* migrate to another consciousness "we should each time change our world."[24] "I've become so accustomed to living in 'my own universe' that I haven't much idea of what's strange or familiar to others."[25] He felt discomfort when meeting a stranger, "because his universe is closed to mine"; the other "seems to shatter unity and the silence of the world for me."[26] As each individual has his own world, so each would have his own religion.[27] God himself deals with us as we are, so he is "pluri-providential," that is, there are "as many independent providences as there are worlds."[28] Though we are radically separate, the pluri-providential God is working to bring these many souls together into a single Soul, the Soul of the World.

In the meantime, we each sum up "the world" in our own way, and it is in this individualist context that one can understand how Teilhard spoke of the salvation of the world. "In each soul, God loves and partly saves the whole world which that soul sums up in an incommunicable and particular way."[29] Likewise in his personal journal he wrote: "To save one's soul is to save the Cosmo-genesis."[30] The world saved by God is the world summed up in an individual mind *(esprit)*, the world one can call "my universe." Salvation comes to the world that has been summed up as someone's mind/spirit. By research one enlarges one's world and that is the basic reason Teilhard regarded research to be of fundamental importance—otherwise some of *the* world would be lost.

When Teilhard first made his reversal, he had difficulty understanding how humans fit into the picture, as each formed a separate world. But during the war he saw troops moving together with a common goal and had vivid intuitions of a higher Soul drawing the troops together. But such intuitions were rare and it took many years for him to integrate this understanding into the rest of his thought. Most of the above quotes telling of separate worlds are from his earlier writings. Near the end of his life he would reflect back on the times he wrote "The Mass on the World" (1923) and *The Divine Milieu* (1926–27) and say "their writing belong to that somewhat self-centered and self enclosed period of my interior life."[31]

The second element that many familiar with Teilhard do not recognize is his idealism. Idealism has taken many forms; the idealism of Teilhard would claim ideas are *more real* than physical objects, but physical objects still retain some reality.[32] When Teilhard first wrote of his reversal in "Cosmic Life," he told of finding support among "idealist thinkers." This continued into his later writings.[33] However, Teilhard would disagree with those idealists who in so valuing mind over matter deny human death, a claim he saw in Christian Science.[34] While some contemporary physicists could be called reductionists, other physicists could be called idealists. The reversal of Teilhard could be seen as a turn from reductionism toward an idealism. Teilhard saw additional support for his idealism in the claims of some modern physicists that their reason was unable to detect in the atoms "anything but the forms that it had itself imposed on them."[35] For Teilhard this meant that the old realism of physics was passing and being replaced by a "scientific idealism."[36] He often developed his ideas in conversation with Edouard Le Roy, a philosopher commonly considered an idealist. Teilhard believed Le Roy had a fine and true worldview, but a "cloudy and provoking metaphysics," one that did not recognize matter as having any existence.[37]

This preference for mind over matter is evident in *The Phenomenon of Man*, which Teilhard sees involving two assumptions. The first of these is "the primacy accorded to the psychic and to thought in the stuff of the universe."[38] Mindful of this primacy, the book tells of "the ultimately psychic nature of evolution."[39] Because mind is more real than matter, Teilhard believed that the human task involves "spiritualizing matter."[40] And matter is spiritualized *when it is perceived,* for then it becomes mind; in mind and as mind (spirit) the object known has a greater reality than it did when it was simply matter. Accordingly, "fuller being is to be found...in the increasing domination of the world by Thought."[41] Because thought is more real than matter, he would claim one should "give things their highest possible degree of being in his knowledge of them."[42] This explains the great value Teilhard placed on scientific research. The things we know constitute our mind, and there they have a *greater* reality than they have in themselves. This is not the ordinary way of understanding the situation. Today people commonly see the physical world as the great reality and their own thoughts as airy nothings (ultimately, this could imply a reductionism). Such was Teilhard before his reversal. After the reversal, matter was seen as the airy nothing (still real) and thought or mind as the greater reality.

Even though many people claim that physical things are more "real" than thoughts, most of these same people value things of the mind more than physical objects. For example: what others "think" of me, or whether someone loves me still seem the important questions. This shows the value we put on "thoughts" and lets us know how real we find them. The Gospels, likewise, are more concerned with what is in the mind than with external fact: "These people honor me with their lips, but their heart is far from me," "Rend your hearts and not your garments." A fellow scientist who worked with Teilhard in the field recalled him explaining that the "workings of the mind are just as truly parts of experience, and hence just as 'real'...as facts that can be proven in the laboratory."[43] The matter was of considerable importance for Teilhard: "My whole outlook is governed increasingly by this physical realness of thought, which is stronger than (or rather includes in its own self) all the boundless properties that a century of research has attributed to matter."[44] Whereas reductionists would reduce all thought to the actions of matter, Teilhard tended to see matter as less real than thought. Such was his moderate "idealism."

Though Teilhard could be called an idealist, he spoke of an "instinctive predilection for matter" and of "feeling at home only when immersed in an ocean of matter." He spoke of matter as holy and even wrote a "Hymn to Matter." But, immediately after telling of his reversal, he dismissed matter as being on the border of nothingness and years later in 1934 claimed, "Matter no longer exists"!![45] Though matter was left on the border of nothingness—or over the border—it still was praised, for it is "a reservoir of spirit."[46] Spirit rises from matter in scientific research, that is, in being known matter become mind/spirit. In the laboratory the scientist does a work of analysis, that is, he or she breaks things down into their component parts (and in a sense materializes them). So Teilhard sees the analytic work of the scientist as moving away from divine realities.[47] But it is only by first doing analysis that the scientist can reverse and enlarge his or her synthesis, a synthesis in the mind. For Teilhard, the theory in the mind is more real than the physical objects that can be said to "obey" the theory. Such was his idealism.

The more comprehensive the synthesis, the more Teilhard would see it reaching a higher level of being. So he saw the universe as presently coming into being; creation was not simply an event of the past but an ongoing reality; creation now continues "at the highest levels of the world"[48]—the level of mind, the primary reality. The world could be seen as moving from a reductionist past toward an idealist future. In Teilhard's terms, the world is being "transformed into Thought"; it is being "metamorphosed into Psyche."[49] In more vivid terms, a journal entry affirms, "The universe transforms itself into an Idea";[50] this happens as it becomes known. The value of material things lies in their ability to become thought while matter serves as the "reservoir" for mind/spirit. Our mind is essentially a process; it is the act of matter becoming thought. "Everything in the world is for Spirit/Mind." *The Phenomenon of Man* even claims that the "consummation of things is bound up with the explicit perception we make of them."[51] "For the stuff of the cosmos, its higher form of existence and its final state of equilibrium lie in *being thought*."[52] But it does not end in perception, for the mind is endlessly working over and "elaborating the essence and totality of the universe deposited within him."[53] This is evolution today or creation continuing "at the highest levels." This work of comprehending the world and thereby raising its level of being takes place *in us* and *as us*. Again, Teilhard's idealism. Yet, in a sense, it is not an idealism. Rather, the physical world that takes on a higher identity in becoming mind would still be termed physical. Our knowledge of physical things is the higher reality that things have attained, but they remain physical.

Our task is "the spiritualization of the universe," and this is accomplished preeminently by scientific research. Thus, research is termed "a vital human function," "the solemn, prime and vital occupation of man, now adult."[54] Research must begin with an idea, a hypothesis, a tentative unity. One must then test the hypothesis in the world of matter. But the scientist in turning to matter does not seek to dissolve in it as if the foundation of the universe were material (this was Teilhard before his reversal). Now one goes to matter *with an idea in mind* (having an idea in mind would not be acceptable for the Buddhist seeking Nirvana); the scientist goes to matter with the intention of returning again to the hypothesis, knowing it has been verified, has been falsified, or is in need of modification. In this back-and-forth process, the universe enters into the human mind and gains a new unity in the form of a greater understanding. This is "the spiritualization of the universe"; it is the universe becoming ideas. By research, matter is becoming mind. As the mind gropes to a more comprehensive understanding, the hypothesis in the mind includes ever more data. In mind and as mind the universe is gaining a unity that is new. "To think 'the world' (as physics is beginning to realize) is not merely to register it but to confer on it a form of unity it would otherwise (i.e. without being thought) be without."[55] Teilhard speaks of the process by analogy:

> The labour of seaweed as it concentrates in its tissues the substances scattered, in infinitesimal quantities, throughout the vast layers of the ocean; the industry of bees as they make honey from the juices broadcast in so many flowers—these are but pale images of the ceaseless working-over that all the forces of the universe undergo in us in order to reach the level of spirit.[56]

Note that "all the forces of the universe" are being worked over and thus reach the level of spirit. This working-over brings about the cosmos as spirit—the cosmos within us. This is the first or natural phase: "Everything in the cosmos is for Spirit." As the mind works on what it finds, the world gains a new unity. We are obligated to develop this inner unity: "we must constantly introduce more and more unity into our ideas."[57] And the creation of the world continues with each advance in human understanding;[58] it continues "at the highest levels" in the world of mind.[59] Again, Teilhard's idealism, an idealism that gives primacy to mind, yet needs matter so that the mind/spirit may develop. Mind can be seen as the higher state matter attains.

To speak of things-becoming-mind *in us* or *as us* implies a different understanding than is generally assumed. For Teilhard, the thing itself is seen as acquiring a second identity in the one who knows it. He is explicit on the point. "Every being has two existences": one is the existence it has in itself, and the other is the existence it has in the minds of those who know it. And because of the primacy of mind, a being is constituted "more by its beyond-self than by its own center."[60] The "beyond-self" could be seen as the influence one has. For example, Teilhard considers Mary the mother of Jesus: she had an original historical reality, but since her death she has taken on a second reality in the minds of Christian peoples.[61] This would be her reality "beyond-self"; and beyond self she remains active. But objects and places also take on a second existence in the mind. Teilhard spoke of the whole European "world [as] living and growing unseen in the depths of [his] being,"[62] and he told of the "Paris within me" summoning him to return—for Teilhard that summons is part of the reality of Paris. Teilhard worked with ancient fossils, and in his mind the fossils took on a life of their own; in him they had become spirit. One could say that his mind kept working over the fossils like the seaweed works over what it gathers from the sea; but it could be put another way: in his mind the fossils seemed to order themselves. They would align themselves differently until suddenly they "fit" and *he* had a new insight—it just came to him! The mind labors to unify what it knows and thus raise it further as spirit.

The mind also labors to understand the people it knows. Teilhard knew a wide variety of people and they too were elements that his mind tried to unify—laboring to understand them as the seaweed labors with what it has taken in. People, and especially their aspirations, continued to live in his mind and affect his thoughts. The authors he read did the same: "Plato and Augustine are still expressing, through me, the whole extent of their personalities."[63] This is their "second existence" in Teilhard—or in humanity; the ideas of Plato and Augustine have become part of the way many people think today; they still influence the way people act. But these philosophers and other authors who have formed our minds do not always agree. Their conflicting claims can leave us divided and uncertain.

> In our intelligence and in our will, we thought that we were extremely simple and very much masters of ourselves. Now, instead of that, we find with horror that we are made of all sorts of fibres…fibres that come from every quarter and from very far afield, each with its own history and life—fibres that are always ready to escape from our control and unravel.[64]

The fibers are the people, ideas, and events that stay with us and sometimes weave into new patterns and sometimes unravel. They make opposing demands; they "meet or conflict with one another."[65] So Teilhard would tell of "the universe battling deep down in our wills."[66] We have received into ourselves the conflicts of the universe; now they are our conflicts. By the presence of others within our mind, we might feel guilty for no good reason or feel pressed to do things we would prefer not to do.

Teilhard tells of making an inner journey: "At each step of the descent a new person was disclosed within me of whose name I was no longer sure, and who no longer obeyed me."[67] These new persons were thinking more or less independently of what his conscious mind was thinking. But objects affected him in much the same way: he told of standing on a rock pile in Asia and finding it was no longer himself thinking, but the earth acting within him, and this he preferred.[68] He would set out to write an essay and find "a spiritual urge has been trying to express itself in me…I feel, indeed, that it is not I that has conceived this essay; it is a someone within me that is greater than I."[69] "I feel too that all the world is living and growing unseen in the depths of my being."[70] He could no longer call his life his own; "It is no longer the atom [the human individual] which lives, but the universe within it."[71] The divided world around us has become mind or spirit in us, but in the process we have become the divided world. At the same time, we feel we have been given a sacred mission to bring a unity to all we have found, to "get it all together." This is the mission that has called many into science—a great work of unification.

Over a period of many years, Teilhard moved from his individualism to a stronger awareness of a common Soul, and as he did he came to give greater importance to scientific research. For the common Soul would be needing a common mind/spirit wherein people can be one. This is what science attempts to do, to give humanity a common way of understanding. Each individual makes some sense of the world and gives it some unity, while science is an effort to develop a unified view that is common for all. Scientific research develops a common mind for a united humanity. Just as Teilhard saw Christ as a single Soul for the universe, he saw science developing a single Mind to go with that Soul. He would claim: "They are (at least partially) right who situate the crown of evolution in a supreme act of collective vision obtained by a pan-human effort of investigation and construction."[72] They are only partially right as they have not seen the divine *Someone* Teilhard would see at the center of it all.

III. The Individual Turns to Prayer

In Teilhard's first essay, which told of his responding to the call of the universe, he asked, "What change is there in the man who has allowed the cares of, and consciousness of, the cosmos to form part of his interior life?"[73] He responds that our own lives lose their central importance, and we have "to accept a supreme renunciation."[74] There is a loss of "ego-centrism" and we become "radiant with selflessness."[75] We feel within ourselves the burdens of others, and in the process we develop "a heart more widely receptive" to the cosmos and other people.[76]

Many found in Teilhard a sympathetic listener and discovered their faith was strengthened in hearing him speak or talking with him one on one. He found their dependence on him both a consolation and a burden. For having a "heart more widely receptive" can leave us taking in more than we can manage. We would like to get our own life together, only to find others burden us with their trials and make demands on our emotions. Perhaps we protest that we have had enough and cannot cope with what we have. And if we are open to others we cannot cope, cannot "get it all together." Being open to others makes our own life more difficult. The universe is reaching out for its soul, and it finds a limited soul in us. People reach out to us to give us their burden, and often they experience relief as their burden becomes ours. And thus the restless universe enters into us, but it is not simply reaching *to* us, it is attempting to reach *through* us for a Soul that comprehends more than we ever can. Only God can act as the final Soul of the World, only God can unify the aspirations of the world. We have been centering the world around ourselves; we have been animating our world, giving it a soul, but it becomes too much. The time comes when we must de-center our world by surrendering it to a greater Soul; this is the act of faith wherein we turn our world over to God. This is the world's salvation, and our own. This is the second step of the two-step process: "Everything that is Spirit is for Christ." Like seaweed, I have summed up the universe as myself, but the summary remains incomplete and starkly finite. The summaries of each must now become Christ— the Summary of summaries. Teilhard often quoted Paul's letter to the Ephesians, which speaks of Christ summing up *(anakephalaiosasthai)* everything on earth and in heaven (Eph 1:10). This is Christ, the Soul of the World, the one in whom "all things hold together" (Col 1:17).

I labor to give a certain unity/soul to my world, but the unity remains limited and incomplete and the fibers of my being are in conflict and sometimes unravel. Teilhard often felt distraught for long periods of time. All the while others were turning to him for guidance and support. He protested, "I am a poor, groping man, fighting too much for his own light and life. I am not a God. What can I do to help them? What comforts me is to think that this internal experience of my weakness is probably my best chance of success. After all, my *'fonction'* is not to bring life to Man, but to show him a little better where Life is coming from."[77] He hoped to show others the way to Christ, for only there would the world gain its final unity, Christ, the one "in whom all things hold together." This turning of one's world over to Christ is the second step of the process: "Everything in Mind/Spirit is for Christ." The time has come for the one open to the world, the one in research, to make an act of faith.

If we are able to turn our world over to Christ, everything changes. We feel freed of a great burden, the burden of being God, of animating everyone and everything around us. By making the act of faith many find they are suddenly able to cope with life. That is because "their universe" has taken its second step and passed through them into Christ. Then one "is able to say literally to God that one loves him, not only with all one's body, all one's heart and all one's soul, but with every fibre of the unifying universe."[78] The act of faith gives "our world" its Soul. And, if I believe, my world looks different. "Our universe," the universe within us, labors to unify itself in an act of understanding—but this will always be vastly incomplete. By the act of faith our world makes contact with the final unity it will have in Christ. By faith, our fragile world has become substantial; it will endure. Graced moments come to us and we can find we are at prayer; for Teilhard, it is the universe, our universe, praying within us. We are the place where the universe prays. So one collection of Teilhard's essays is called *The Hymn of the Universe*, and another, *The Prayer of the Universe*. In such moments the myriad of elements that constitute our world are reaching *through* us and finding the consummation they seek in God. We are at prayer. In Teilhard's "Mass on the World," our souls are the paten and chalice, the place where our world rests; then, by faith in the consecration, our world is claimed by God.

This can sound esoteric, but it is not. It can even enable Christians to understand better how they pray the psalms. Many psalms have passages like, "Praise him, sun and moon, praise him, all you shining stars. Praise him, you highest heavens, and you waters above the heavens" (Ps 148:3–4). But having exhorted the sun and moon to say their prayers, what do we expect them to do? *In themselves* the sun is a ball of fire and the moon is a rock—objects not known for devotion. But beyond the physical being they have in themselves the sun and the moon have a second existence within me, an existence as mind or spirit, and as such they can be restless and at times they can exalt. When I feel them about to exalt I can encourage the process, "Sun and moon, bless the Lord! Snow and hail, bless the Lord!" And the world (the world as it is in me) exalts in God. Perhaps the beauty of the earth gives my heart a joy that it cannot contain. Yet I was not meant to contain it, for the world is reaching through me for an opening into God. If I "believe," if I make an act of faith, the world that has entered me passes beyond me to its consummation. With wonder I experience the process as beauty, for I seem to see Another greater than I animating all things. Beauty brings relief to my troubled soul. All things appear filled with a meaning beyond what I give them: "It is in one single movement that Nature grows in beauty and the Body of Christ reaches its full development."[79]

But the world in us does more than rejoice; there are times when the world we know is rent by pain and sorrow. Our pain, the pain of our friends, the pain of the world, each has become spirit in us, and this too becomes more than we can bear; it too seeks to pass through us to God. A passage from St. Paul could illustrate: "We know that the whole creation groans together in travail even until now"; the creation is groaning because of its "bondage to decay" (Rom 8:22–24). *In itself* the creation is not groaning; in themselves rocks and trees never do that. But there are times I seem to hear all creation groaning in travail; it is the creation as spirit groaning in me and *its* groans constitute the troubled prayer I offer. The universe is weeping within me, and its pain can rise through me to God. The hymn of the universe is often a cry of pain; that too is found in the psalms. But in praying the psalms, I gain some relief; for even the cry of pain can be experienced as beauty.

The pain of those we love takes us beyond ourselves and this gives us a wider basis for prayer. The world of Teilhard included a sister very dear to him, Marguerite-Marie, who was crippled for many years with tuberculosis of the spine. After her death in 1936 he wrote a tribute to her:

> O Marguerite, my sister, while I, given body and soul to the positive forces of the universe, was wandering over continents and oceans...you lay motionless, stretched out on your bed of sickness; silently, deep within yourself, you were transforming into light the world's most grievous shadows. In the eyes of the Creator, which of us, tell me, which of us will have had the better part?[80]

She was transforming her world into light, while he was transforming his. Each was "given" a different world and each was spiritualizing the world given him or her. His world included her and her world included him, yet they were different worlds. This was the natural part of the process. The supernatural part depended on what she and he would make of things, their free decisions. They could become bitter and turn in on themselves as their entire world reflects their bitterness; but they could also let the world pass through them into the great Soul of the World. And their world would rejoice. The first step is the natural step of experience (research); it is done in one way by Teilhard the scientist and in another by Marguerite stretched out in pain. The second step concerns what they do—or what we do—with the joys and the pains that come in life. We must choose between "arrogant autonomy and excentration,"[81] and, if we chose excentration, our world will pass beyond us. This is adoration; the world centered on us becomes centered on Another who is greater.[82]

"In the act in which I decide to give myself to God I pass altogether...with all the nuances and all the detail of my past."[83] Many events of my past stay with me and constitute my world.

Following a visit to a friend, Teilhard wrote, "I am still living those three weeks."[84] The "three weeks" refers to an earlier time when he and his friend had several valuable conversations. Such times remain within us and give us life, while other moments live within and take life away. If I am able to give myself to God, the past takes on a different meaning. The frustrations I have known are seen as steps that have brought me to faith. If I believe, I see a different world. Everything *looks* different; everything appears luminous. My world has changed.

> If we believe, then everything is illuminated and takes shape around us: chance is seen to be order, success assumes an incorruptible plenitude, suffering becomes a visit and a caress of God. But if we hesitate, the rock remains dry, the sky dark, the waters treacherous and shifting.[85]

We know from experience how much our world depends on what we believe about it (again showing the great reality of thought). So Teilhard speaks of faith as an operative power, for in making the act of faith my world is changed. If I have a living faith, I live a bright and supporting world centered on God. Then everything that happens to me is *seen* as the loving action of Christ; events are felt as a touch of his hand; they seem to be animated by One who is greater than I, by the great World Soul. But if I refuse to believe and see decay and entropy as the end of all things, the world I live seems dead and all action without point; things are *seen* to be heading to death. Without faith, whatever happens seems arbitrary and unfair; I am a victim of chance. But, if I believe, the entirety of the world I know lights up, for I see it reaching its consummation in Christ; the poison of universal death "has vanished from the heart of all things."[86] By our faith, things are "profoundly modified in our eyes"; "the divine must flood into the universe, in so far as the universe is centered on me."[87] Everything looks alive. In me and through me it attains its salvation. The world once seen as marked for death (my world) has been delivered, and I see all things differently.

The first time a man says, "I believe," nothing outside his own soul appears to alter. In fact, through the words he has spoken, that man has produced a reaction in universal Reality. Hardly has he given his assent to revealed Truth, before all created powers are transformed, as though by magic, *in the circle of which he is the center.* Natural forces, hitherto alien, hostile or ambivalent, are without exception straightaway charged for him with the influence of Christ…the whole impact of things…brings a contact with Christ; he feels in them the touch of Christ's hand.[88]

Things, while retaining their habitual texture, seem to be made out of a different substance. Everything remains the same as far as phenomena are concerned, but at the same time everything becomes luminous, animated, instinct with love. Through the operation of faith, Christ appears.[89]

Christ "appears," for now "my universe" is seen to be animated by a great and loving Soul other than my own. This vision of Christ was so vivid, that Teilhard claimed he "must live only to develop *spirituality in immediacy*"[90]—a spirituality centered on the act of perception. Sometimes his writing can seem highly abstract, yet he insisted that he speaks of what is "concrete." He wanted to tell of Christ "in some way 'immediately apprehended.'" The world that is seen to be Christ is the world that is saved—my world and your world, if we believe. This has happened in two steps; in the first step the world has entered into us to become mind/spirit. In the second, the world passes beyond us into Christ. This is the "gradual incorporation of the world into the Word incarnate."[91] Through the long ages, Christ is becoming the one in whom all things will hold together (see Col 1:17).

In all these passages Teilhard is speaking of the "world" in an unaccustomed way. At the basis of this original way of speaking his world-as-spirit could be seen more or less as what is called the subconscious or unconscious mind. Rather than our seeing this as simply part of our self, Teilhard would speak of it as *the world dwelling within us*, the world as spirit—the "spirit of the earth." This "spirit of the earth" is apart from the conscious mind and often acts independently of our conscious decisions. So in his inner journey: "At each step of the descent a new person was disclosed within me of whose name I was no longer sure and who no longer obeyed me."[92] St. Augustine would speak of spirit as that which is *in nobis sine nobis*, in us without being us. And Teilhard would quote St. Augustine's Latin on many occasions.[93] St. Augustine's phrase tells of the ambiguity of spirit—it is both one's self and other than one's self. In Teilhard's speaking of it as the world (world become spirit in us), he stresses the otherness of its character. Thus, people I have known, people I have loved, people who annoy me, all are with me still; they are present as *spirit*. They affect the way I think and my ability to pray.

I might set out to pray and find I do not get there. Perhaps it is because a cynical "spirit" is within me and as I begin to pray it asks, "What do you think you are doing?" and I am drawn into an argument. The voice is that of someone whom I respect or care for, or perhaps only one whom I know in a general way, and this other might think prayer is nonsense. Knowing what a cynic thinks can hinder my prayer. Feeling a bond with those who reject prayer or respecting their judgment can change our ability to pray: it can make prayer easier if those who mean something to us are faith-filled believers, and more difficult if they are not. Aware of this, many people look for a faith community, one that believes as they do, and this supports their prayer. Beyond that, it can be troubling to know there are others who do not share one's faith at all. Perhaps this difficulty in prayer has given rise to forced conversions and the killing of infidels. For if everyone could agree and there were no nonbelievers, my prayer could be more complete—there would be no alien voices challenging me. Teilhard claimed that for religion to be complete, "there cannot be any other subject than the totality of thought on earth."[94] Likewise, I find my religion incomplete as long as others do not agree with me. I cannot pray with a whole mind, a whole heart, and a whole soul. A similar belief seems to underlie a passage from a novel of Dostoyevsky:

> [The Grand Inquisitor is speaking.] For these pitiful creatures are concerned not only to find what one or the other can worship; what is essential is that all may be together in it. This craving for community of worship is the chief misery of every man, individually and of all humanity from the beginning of time. For the sake of common worship they've slain each other with the sword.[95]

But how can anyone's worship be complete today when everyone knows we live in a pluralistic world? To set the issue in terms of Teilhard: faith involves more than a decision of the conscious mind; it involves the pluralistic world that is spirit in us. Can a pluralistic spirit pray at all? Today, more than in previous ages, we find ourselves to be pluralist, and this can leave us unable to pray, for, as Teilhard would have it, "there cannot be any other subject [of religious belief] than the totality of thought on earth." Presently there is no such totality. So our prayer seems essentially incomplete. "Our individual mystical effort awaits an essential completion in its union with the mystical efforts of all other men."[96] In other terms, Teilhard writes, "The organ made for seeing God is not...the isolated human soul; it is the human soul united to all the other souls."[97] But today all human souls are not united. Then how can God be seen today without an organ for seeing him and with a divided humanity?

The ways of dealing with different inner spirits (different ways the world has entered us) have been considered abundantly in the Christian tradition. One way of resolving the issue has consisted in making one's self indifferent to all created things: "empty one's self of the world." Then, when no creature engages us, we might freely and completely turn to our Creator; that is, when all created lights are extinguished, the Light of God can shine. Thomas Merton (quoting St. Bonaventure) wrote: "*Ipsa caligo summa est mentis illuminatio.*"[98] "The height of darkness is the mind's Illuminatio"; when the light of all creatures has been darkened, one is illumined by the uncreated Light. For Merton, to darken the light of all creatures, we must purify our hearts of all attachments to the world, becoming indifferent to all created things—including all people. Many in knowing this ideal felt called to leave their family and the city for the hermitage. This move to disinterest is found in many Christian devotional texts: a fourteenth-century work called *The Cloud of Unknowing* advises: "Try to forget all created things that he [God] ever made, and the purpose behind them, so that your thought and longing do not turn or reach out to them." The work advises that we put a cloud of forgetting between ourselves and all creatures.[99] This spirituality was presented most forcefully by St. John of the Cross (Teilhard often refers to him in this context). In the sixteenth century, St. John spoke of going to God by eliminating all desire and coming to the Darkness that is Light; this involves an immense purification, the ascent of Mt. Carmel. Such an ascent is even suggested in the writings of St. Ignatius Loyola, the founder of the Jesuits (Teilhard's community). St. Ignatius wanted one to be indifferent to health or sickness, riches or poverty, a long life or a short life, and so forth. To be indifferent suggests that one be without desire for these or anything but God. Teilhard knew this spirituality constituted a large part of the Christian tradition, but he considered it an ideal for Buddhists, not Christians: "The Buddhist denies himself to kill desire (he does not believe in the value of being). While the authentic Christian makes the same gesture by a superabundance of desire and of faith in the value of being."[100] Thus, Teilhard acknowledges that there is still the need for mortification, but the mortification is not to kill all desire; it is oriented to discovering within one's self "a desire as vast as the universe," a desire so great that only Christ as Soul of the universe can satisfy. Teilhard found "the capacity of Our Lord to save human aspirations" to be a proof of his divinity.[101] Christian mortification still has its place, for it enables us to set aside trivial desires and so encounter our fundamental desire; it is a matter of saying a thousand small nos in order to say the great Yes. And our Yes brings our cosmos to its consummation.

For Teilhard, the Christian should not seek to enjoy creatures in themselves, but "so that he might extract all the essence of beauty and spirituality that they contain and return these qualities to God."[102] In retaining his love of creatures, Teilhard was aware his claims were at odds with a large part of the Christian tradition. Therefore, when he finished writing his first essay ("Cosmic Life") he added a note to acknowledge the difference. The different ascesis he proposed is most evident in the words of dedication he set at the begining of *The Divine Milieu:* "For those who love the world." There is a long Christian tradition claiming that the one who loves the world cannot love God, for one cannot serve two masters. But for Teilhard, love of the world initiates us into a greater love, and, if we are sensitive to it, it will eventually lead us to a Love greater than the world can satisfy. Likewise, by working with the limited truths of science, we will be led to the Truth that is greater than science can know. Yet to attain to infinite Love and infinite Truth, we must begin with "the love that initiates and the truth that passes away."[103]

Thomas Merton told of going to the monastery to quiet the seven guys who argued in his head. His early writings tell abundantly of rejecting the world and gaining a peace the world cannot give. But if one continues to love the world—as Teilhard proposed—will not that leave one filled with a babble of conflicting voices, conflicting spirits? Then in going to prayer would not the nonbelievers who have a place in our hearts come forth to interfere with our prayer? With Teilhard the answer is both No and Yes.

The No would claim Teilhard did not find love for the world and its people an obstacle to his prayer, and often this was the case. He believed that both believers and nonbelievers were not able to state directly what they desired. Yet in listening to them, he seemed to hear them saying the same thing. Psychologists speak of "listening with the Third Ear" (listening for a message hidden behind what is stated explicitly). For example, the psychologist does not accept the dreams of his or her patients at face value, nor many of their other claims. Teilhard had a wide variety of friends, some churchmen, some scientists, some Communists, some Americans, some Asians, and so forth. But in talking with them he came to believe that, in spite of the difference in cultures and personal statements, they were all seeking one thing: union with the All: "Man is not drawn to the One (that is, the Whole [*le Tout*]) by his reason alone, but by the full force of his whole being."[104] In his first essay, "Cosmic Life," he told of the force of this drive for union. At first he sought union by attempting to dissolve into matter. Then, he made a reversal, but continued to seek this union, now in a common Soul. But by his reversal it was no longer a union in which differences are dissolved; it was a *communion* in which differences are deepened. All people were calling for a love that would embrace humanity in a community— such as the community he had known with his fellow soldiers in the war when he and they felt animated by a common Soul. This community would include the whole of creation. He believed all people were seeking to escape their isolation and come to a loving union with the All, all things united in a great communion. Their stated concerns might vary sharply, but beneath their words they were all expressing a fundamental "aspiration" for this union. In listening to others he seemed to hear this single message beneath their words.

But this single aspiration was not always immediately evident; as the war ended Teilhard told of going into the cathedral in Strasbourg, "and beneath its dim vaults I try to introduce a little more order into the world of aspirations—still in spite of everything, very confused—I feel within myself."[105] He had just known the exaltation of victory and crowds of Alsatians in the streets wildly cheering the arrival of the French army. This gave him a new sense of human "aspirations" and new material to order in his mind and hear as a call for unity. He knew others would be puzzled by his "forever seeking something *behind themselves*."[106] For he listened intently to others. He listened "with the Third Ear" for the fundamental hunger for unity "behind" the words they said.

Was he onto something? The present author has spoken with many who knew Teilhard and believed they knew him *well*.

Lita Osmundsen, who managed the Wenner-Gren when Teilhard was working there in the years just before his death, said Teilhard had an ongoing problem with people thinking they were his closest friend: "For he listened to everyone so intently, it was as if there were no one else in the world." He was listening for something (a mystical aspiration) deep within the other's speech, a hunger he knew well and to which he believed he had something to say. But first he had to listen and discover the form this hunger had taken in them; then he would speak to them accordingly. And many felt they were understood as never before. The present author never met Teilhard, but in reading only a few pages of *The Divine Milieu* felt he was being addressed more directly than he was by any other author. Others have told of similar experiences in reading Teilhard. And there is no doubt Teilhard was encouraged by the "contagious power" his ideas seemed to have. When he spoke to their aspirations for communion, they responded so that he knew of followers "ranging from the border-line of unbelief to the depths of the cloister—thinking and feeling, or at least beginning vaguely to feel, just as I do."[107] He believed they were all yearning for "something greater than us," a "yearning for total union." This yearning seemed to be all about him, so he spoke of it poetically as "the voice of the single soul of the ages to come, weeping in us for its Multitude."[108] He too was part of weeping humanity, and the other voices within him could unite in their yearning. Feeling this universal support—though differently expressed—he felt no need to slay infidels for interfering with his prayer. For in "listening with the Third Ear," he heard them and himself, unbelievers and believers, calling for a Soul that would unite them. Likewise, he felt no need for an asceticism that would eliminate his feelings for others (and for the world), for he believed all humanity shared the same hunger. Within him these hungers would constitute the immensity of his own desire. So "the capacity of Our Lord to save human aspirations" was seen as a proof of Christ's divinity.

But beyond saying others did not interfere with his prayer, there was also the fact that others *did* interfere with his prayer. As a young priest before the war he told of visiting the caves at

Altamira in Spain where stone-age paintings were on the ceiling. He tried to understand what the paintings meant to the cave artists and found it "quite disturbing"; he decided not to return to the caves.[109] To what did these artists aspire? Were they really seeking unity? Then again, in first going to Asia he told of losing his moral footing in seeing civilizations that had never known Christ. The Chinese seemed wholly given to the practical with no mystical aspiration, and in great anxiety Teilhard kept seeking "some corner in the Chinese mind" open to mysticism. Later he visited the cyclotrons at Berkeley and his Jesuit friend Pierre Leroy said he was shaken to the core.[110] He had troubles with anxiety all his life, especially in his final years. Many of his troubles developed out of his inability to integrate what he saw into "his world," a world centered on the claim that everyone aspired to a single Soul. In meeting people who seemed to have no such aspiration, Teilhard was troubled personally: "all the strain and struggle of the universe reach down into the most hidden places of my being."[111] Many people who suffer from depression and anxiety seem to have taken on themselves "the strain and struggle of the universe." Many such people develop a philosophical turn that does not concern more practical people; such people feel obliged to make sense of things that others ignore.

In his first essay after telling of his reversal, Teilhard told of a "widening of his desires" and wondered, "What change is there in the man who has allowed the cares of, and consciousness of, the cosmos to form part of his interior life?"[112] Part of the answer came to him in bouts of anxiety and depression.

Sometimes after a struggle he would integrate the disturbing elements into his world and then he vividly sensed the divine Presence. The *esprits* troubling him had found their way to God. He often spoke of such moments as a "conquest"; mind had gained its ascendency over the confusion of experience, and in the process more of the world had become unified as mind/spirit. In first going to Asia he wrote, "I am not able to *dominate* and assimilate this mass of impressions undergone rapidly and superficially." Rather, "I am especially *dominated by* the confused impression of the human world...it is an immense and disparate thing."[113] Some people speak of it as a need to get on top of things, to regain control. Other people gain so much control that they are open to no one and seem more mechanical than alive—the world of such people seems so limited. For Teilhard the ideal was to be *in the process of coming into control,* but to be in this process he had to receive continually into himself troubling things beyond his comprehension, and that involved an ongoing struggle to unify. He felt committed to research, for the one who does research is at the place where the mind struggles to bring disordered experience into a unified understanding. But sometimes in the struggle, one is "*dominated by* the confused impressions" of a senseless chaos and one becomes anxious. We must be brought "forcefully up against the separateness and antagonism of the cosmic elements before we can be enthralled by the feeling of their underlying solidarity."[114] In a similar way, those troubled by anxiety attacks often feel their depression is a necessary part of their knowing the exaltation of a new understanding. Teilhard wrote in his journal: "The more an idea is subversive, the more it is powerful (rich with truth), the more it is Christianizable."[115]

But apart from difficulties he encountered in his research, Teilhard knew similar anxieties through his friendships with women. Shortly before beginning his military service (he was in his early thirties) and until his death forty years later, he was fascinated by a series of women and they were fascinated by him. But he believed he was called to be a celibate priest, so he had difficulty fitting women—many of them very independent-minded— into "his world." Yet he found such women drew him out of himself and into a fuller life. They seemed to inspire his writings, so he kept their company and expressed his affection for them. All available evidence indicates that he was faithful to his religious vows. In such relationships he believed that both the woman's soul and his could rise to God. (He explained the process to the women he knew.) Again, the understanding had to begin with a disturbing experience (women disturbed his commitment to chastity), but this was what he must overcome by a "conquest." He wrote to Lucile Swan: "I can enjoy more directly the joy and the strength of our mutual and common conquests. Because, really, the meaning of our friendship is to discover and to con-quer,—ourselves, each other, and the great world around us."[116] The conquest is that of mind over matter. And there are times when each person tries to hold onto an understanding of one's self and yet is troubled by fascinations that do not fit with this self-understanding. Teilhard felt a mission to go where his vision would be threatened, for only thus could he enlarge his vision and that meant enlarging the world animated by Christ. He prayed, "Greater still, Lord, let your universe be greater still, so that I may hold you and be held by you by a contact at once made ever more intense and ever wider in its extent!"[117] When he could integrate what he found into his vision, he felt joy and confirmation; when he could not he was given to anxiety and depression.

Teilhard saw conquest as the movement of life, evolution was forming ever wider syntheses in opposition to the disintegration of entropy. This gave a very positive thrust to his spirituality and made it different than the familiar spiritualities he had studied. He developed this positive orientation while aware of suffering and death: first, while working among the wounded and dying of war; then further in war-torn China and Japanese-occupied Beijing; and all the while his work as a geologist was a study of the bones of the dead. He had come to realize that life had developed and grown only through a "struggle for existence," and that life sur-vived and flourished only upon the death of what had been. Beyond that, he accepted the claims of physicists that all life in the universe would end and order would disintegrate (entropy). Thus, his spirituality, like all spiritualities that preceded his, had to rec-ognize that all things are passing. Henri de Lubac, a Jesuit friend and author of several books on Teilhard, has called all of Teilhard's writings, even his scientific works, one long meditation on death.[118] The long Christian tradition has often suggested death as a subject for meditation. Teilhard would agree and certainly med-itated on it often, but he differed from his predecessors in insist-ing that first there is need for human progress (personal growth, new scientific understandings, better social structures, etc.—in short, conquests); all of these were seen as part of the building work of evolution. But all of these were overshadowed by the inevitability of death, the death of the individual and the death of the cosmos. His spirituality would have it that there are two phases: first, a phase where we must strive with all our might to bring about growth within and without. This is his spirituality of human work. It requires the "fine steel of the human will" to work against the encroaching darkness.[119] But the time comes for everyone when effort is of no avail and diminishment and death is inevitable; at this point, *but not before*, surrender is the will of God. Every diminishment brings us face to face with our limits and only then is it the divine will that we surrender. Like the Christian tradition before him, he saw great value in self-sacrifice, but for such a sacrifice he insisted there must *be a self*. To build the self and the world, he believed that "renunciation and asceticism" still play an all important part[120]—any conquest involves renunciation and asceticism. Then begins the second phase wherein we are to lovingly surrender to the forces that bring us death. That is the time we need the traditional spiritualities.

There is the tradition found in *The Cloud of Unknowing*, St. John of the Cross, and others that calls for a rupture with the natural world. Teilhard did not deny this tradition, but he insisted that before the rupture there must be a time of natural growth.** "Without having a victim, there can be no sacrifice." So he called for conquest, growth, and self-development; "the natural elements are absolutely necessary to this work of salvation."[121] But the self that is developed naturally must come eventually to a rupture, a moment of annihilation. Only after this will it rise to new life. He spoke of it as a *retournement*, that is, a turning inside out. Turning something inside out radically changes it, but it is not the same as coming up with something entirely new. In heaven, we

---

** Contemporary spiritual directors have told of some directees having such a fragile sense of self that the directors must first try to give the directee a minimum of self-confidence. When Thomas Merton became novice director, he was surprised to find this was the need of many novices. The sons of Mahatma Gandhi became alcoholics and his wife reproved him: "You wanted to make our sons holy men before they were men." In each case, self-development must proceed self-sacrifice. This need for self-development is a major theme in Teilhard, but it has not been a theme in much spiritual writing, East or West.

89

will see God with the eyes we have developed on earth. But by the *retournement* we must first pass through a moment of absolute annihilation. To explain this he offered the analogy of one cone on top of another with their two apexes touching at a common point. The lower cone flows into the upper cone so that the upper cone could be said to exist and have its dimensions defined by the lower cone. But for the lower cone to pass into the upper it must first diminish to a point—with an area of zero—and only then expand as the upper cone. In a similar way, we too must diminish and be annihilated.[122] "The supreme salvific transformation of the Universe consists in its conscious annihilation in God."[123] Teilhard used the word *annihilation* on many occasions (it was even seen as a condition of progress[124]). But beyond the annihilation, our self will be radically transformed into our true identity in the divine bosom. Only with death will we be fully united and fully ourselves; that is, we will know in its fullness the union that differentiates.

In an account of his faith writen in 1934, Teilhard wrote as though a radiant and serene future awaited him. Then, in considering what he had written, he was concerned lest one assume he saw death as "simply as one of those periods of sleep after which we can count on seeing the dawn of a glorious new day. The reality is very different."[125] He told of being certain and ever more certain that he must proceed "as though Christ awaited me at the term of the universe," and added, "at the same time I feel no special assurance of the existence of Christ. Believing is not seeing" (note the word *special*). In the annihilation of death one proceeds beyond all seeing, and Teilhard knew the difference. In the private notes that he made during his annual retreats, he sometimes told of a fear that there would be nothing.[126] On one occasion he looked forward to death as the time he would find Christ, and added, "What a thrill!" (He actually uses the English word *thrill*.[127])

Teilhard began as a writer and original thinker by writing "Cosmic Life" and there he told of a summons to join the great All. He was the particle yearning to unite with the Whole and this yearning was seen as the basis of all mysticisms. At first he allowed himself to relax and more or less dissolve into the material world—seeking Nirvana and the absence of desire. But he reversed, made a "complete turn-about," and sought another form of union with the All, a communion in one Soul. He knew moments of this communion, and believed the communion would be complete only on the other side of death. In order to love anyone, one must more or less die to one's self. But total Love demands a total death, annihilation, and beyond that one finds one's self in God. Jesus seems to call us to a radical loss that leads to finding one's self in union: "He who loses himself for my sake and the Gospel will find himself."

We can lose ourselves in our work, work done with a right intention and that contributes to building Christ's body. We further lose ourselves in our diminishments. But the one who is "filled with an impassioned love for Jesus hidden in the forces which bring death to the earth, him the earth will clasp in the immensity of her arms as her strength fails, and with her he will awaken in the bosom of God."[128]

This is a passage from Teilhard's "Mass on the World," and it is only there that such thoughts are fully developed.

Notes

1. HE, 125; MM, 224; HM, 215, 191, 221.
2. Cuenot, 88; J, February 27, 1924.
3. LMF, 196.
4. HM, 216.
5. W, 30.
6. HM, 24.
7. W, 32.
8. W, 30; F, 50, 81, 91, 188; HE, 22, 98; HM, 84; C, 109; T, 114; S, 95; MM, 68; A, 88, 121, 143, 144, 329; P, 52, 271, 272.
9. W, 273; see 1 Cor 15:28; Eph 1:23; Col 3:11; De Lubac; MM, 28–29.
10. LJM, 155.
11. W, 275.
12. W, 179–90. See especially p. 178; it is only in a later essay that he applied the term to Christ.

13. F, 22; MM, 282.
14. HM, 175, 177.
15. F, 23–24.
16. J, August 12, 1924.
17. Li, 223, 245–46; T, 47–52; A, 227.
18. W, 238–39.
19. MM, 240–41.
20. MM, 202.
21. W, 208.
22. LTF, 63.
23. MM, 218.
24. D, 141.
25. MM, 240–41.
26. D, 145.
27. MM, 236.
28. W, 238.
29. D, 60.
30. J, October 21, 1954.
31. HM, 52.
32. See King, 54–61.
33. W, 40, 235–37; MM, 166, 235; C, 51; Li, 92; HE, 114; J, February 19, 1924; UL, Gaudefroy, May 22, 1932.
34. W, 235–37; MM, 235.
35. HE, 174.
36. HE, 114.
37. UL, Breuil, January 16, 1932.
38. P, 30.
39. P, 146.
40. W, 38.
41. S, 81.
42. W, 139.
43. Barbour, 39.
44. LT, 150.
45. C, 105.
46. C, 217.
47. S, 21.
48. D, 62.
49. HM, 28.

50. J, March 25, 1952.
51. P, 249.
52. T, 165; italics in text.
53. P, 180.
54. S, 22; HE, 163.
55. P, 249; parentheses in text.
56. D, 60.
57. T, 117.
58. S, 32.
59. D, 62; P, 249.
60. J, 185; see also J, December 12, 1922; February 19, 1924.
61. J, December 12, 1922.
62. LT, 166.
63. F, 18.
64. A, 188.
65. W, 25.
66. S, 95.
67. D, 77.
68. LTF, 73.
69. S, 38.
70. LT, 166.
71. D, 73.
72. P, 249; he finds this idea in Brunschvig; parentheses in text.
73. W, 41.
74. W, 66.
75. W, 184.
76. W, 70.
77. LS, 181.
78. P, 297; HE, 159; S, 172; HM, 101.
79. W, 62.
80. A, 249.
81. F, 19.
82. See T, 117, 219.
83. Li, 42.
84. UL, Riviere, December 14, 1942.
85. D, 136.
86. A, 401.
87. A, 146; W, 216.

88. W, 257–58.
89. W, 246.
90. MM, 241; emphasis in text.
91. F, 37.
92. D, 77.
93. LTF, 32; D, 49; W, 213; J, 48; UL, Fontoynont, March 15, 1916; UL, Le Roy, January 28, 1934.
94. C, 119.
95. Dos, 301.
96. D, 143.
97. C, 16.
98. Merton, 173.
99. CU, 61, 66.
100. Li, 246; parentheses in text.
101. UJ, April 15, 1925.
102. S, 140.
103. HM, 69.
104. C, 102, 57.
105. MM, 261.
106. HM, 74.
107. HM, 101.
108. W, 101.
109. LP, 85.
110. LMF, 135.
111. W, 215.
112. W, 41.
113. UL, Breuil, May 25, 1923; emphasis added.
114. T, 42.
115. UJ, June 6, 1925.
116. LS, 29.
117. D, 47.
118. De Lubac, RT, 48; De Lubac, TMM, 108.
119. D, 92.
120. See W, 71.
121. Cor, 33.
122. Cor, 33.
123. Nr, 65.
124. LGI, 34.

125. C, 131.
126. Nr, 192, 111.
127. Nr, 223.
128. HM, 130.

5.

A COMMENTARY ON PASSAGES FROM "THE MASS ON THE WORLD"

"Let me explain."

The preceding chapter sketched out the philosophy, theology, and spirituality of Teilhard. This chapter applies what has been said to Teilhard's "Mass."

In both his essays on the Mass—"The Priest" and "The Mass on the World"—Teilhard considers only the sacramental part of the Mass; that is, he begins with the offertory and altogether omits the Liturgy of the Word. Toward the end of his life, he made brief notes during his annual retreat for an essay that would include the Liturgy of the Word, but he never wrote the essay.

"This time not in the forests of the Aisne, but in the steppes of Asia."

In the summer of 1918 Teilhard's regiment was stationed by the Aisne River near Soissons. They awaited the next battle in a forest where vaults of ancient trees stretched above them, and Teilhard could think of no better temple of recollection. Since he lacked what he needed to offer Mass, he developed a spiritual form of the Mass, "The Priest," the twelfth of his nineteen wartime essays. After the war and during demobilization he continued to work on the text and share it with friends. Meanwhile, a French Jesuit missionary in China had been finding old stone tools and invited Teilhard to come to the sites from which they were extracted. On April 6, 1923, Teilhard sailed from Marseilles and, passing through Suez, continued on to India, Ceylon, and the

Moluccas. He walked the streets of Saigon, Hong Kong, and Peking before joining Licent in Tientsin. Soon both left by train to the end of the rail line, where they bought mules and headed into the desert steppes. For long periods they were without what they needed to offer Mass—rubrics then were more demanding—so again lacking bread, wine, and altar (as during the war) *"in the steppes of Asia"* Teilhard developed his spiritual "Mass."

"I...will offer you all the labours and sufferings of the world."

At every Mass there is a double offering, bread and wine. Lacking these, Teilhard offers the labors (bread) and suffering (wine) of the world; later the bread will be the harvest to be won by the day's labor and wine will be the sap pressed from the earth's fruits; the same two are also called the hopes and the miseries of the earth. The harvest is the growth of the world, while the sap is its diminishment. The bread includes all that is about "to spring up, to grow, to flower, to ripen during this day," while the wine is "every death force which waits in readiness to corrode, to wither, to cut down." Teilhard explained in a letter, "The true substance to be consecrated each day is the world's development during that day—the bread symbolizing appropriately what creation succeeds in producing, the wine (blood) what creation causes to be lost in exhaustion and suffering in the course of its effort."[1]

The two elements are the growth and diminishment of which Teilhard often spoke, and they correspond to the two fundamental processes that occur each day in the universe: evolution and entropy. Evolution is the building up of structure and entropy is the breaking down of structure. Scientists claim that the entropy of the universe increases each day, and after billions of years structures will have broken down to such an extent that all life will cease and the universe will pass into its "heat death." But in Teilhard's "Mass" God becomes incarnate in *both* the growth of the world (body) *and* in its diminishments (blood). Through these God will lead the earth beyond diminishment into everlasting life. Teilhard speaks often of God present in the "Becoming" or in "Developments." Both words speak of process, and fundamentally there are two processes, progress and setbacks. And corresponding to these two elements are offered, bread and wine.

With evolution as a move to order and entropy as a move to chaos, two basic movements identified in contemporary science are offered to God daily for consecration in Teilhard's "Mass." Some similarities can be found in many ancient liturgies to the offering and consecration of the *bread,* for often the Lord was seen to bring order out of chaos. Scripture scholars find this theme in the psalms that tell of a divine Enthronement.: "The Lord reigns! Yea, the world is established, it shall never be moved" (Ps 96:10). The world is ordered as God's control is established. This was probably symbolized in the vestments of the Jewish high priest, which had cosmic symbols in imitation of the Babylonians.[2] The Babylonians saw Marduk (order) doing battle with Tiamat (chaos) and emerging victorious ("the world is established"). So the Old Testament book of Genesis tells of creation as God bringing order and form out of chaos ("in the Beginning...the earth was without form and void"). In a similar way for Teilhard, the Lord is bringing about an increasing order in the advance of evolution, and his "Mass" picks up this theme; here Teilhard sees the ordering move of evolution as the process by which Christ forms his body. Thus, Teilhard would not speak of God "having created the world," but as God "creating it still." But, in contrast to the ancient liturgies, Teilhard also saw the move to chaos, death, and entropy (similar to Babylon's Tiamat?) receiving consecration as the blood of Christ. So the tragedies of war and his ongoing personal frustrations were consecrated each day and constituted his communion with the blood of Christ. In this claim, the move to diminishment is only another form of the work of the Lord. An old Christian tradition—more popular than scholarly—would refer to the negative aspects of the divine action as the "left hand of God."

"Over there, on the horizon, the sun has just touched with light the outermost fringe of the eastern sky."

Teilhard always had a strong orientation to the future; here at daybreak he looks forward to the coming day. In 1923, the

Chinese retained an old custom: they would name a foreigner living among them by devising a three-word combination that vaguely suggested to them the sound of the person's name as pronounced in one's own tongue. The three characters by which Teilhard was named were "Father Daybreak Virtue." Beyond that they knew him as "the smiling scientist."[3]

> *"My paten and my chalice are the depths of a soul laid widely open to all the forces."*

The paten and the chalice are the depths *of a soul*—an individual soul; the phrase thus suggests Teilhard's individualism. Yet it is not that simple, for others are contained in that soul as elements to be consecrated. Many friends told Teilhard of their hopes and burdens, and these entered into the depths of his soul where they remained active. Many of the people we have known remain important to us and continue to live within us ("we have found the world in our own souls"[4]). So Teilhard sees himself as the paten containing the growth and hopes of others and the chalice containing their diminishments and pain. But in the offertory he makes their presence within more explicit: *"one by one"* he recalls the people who have affected him. First, he recalls his family, and then wider families that have developed around him, friends and co-workers *"with affinities of the heart, of scientific research, and of thought."* These people constitute his world. By recalling them they become alive within him, that is, their hopes are present on his paten and their pain is in his chalice—the paten and chalice are his soul. We all contain similar elements on our paten and in our chalice.

Some spiritual writers speak of stepping back from all human concerns as we approach the Mass. That way we can better focus on God. To further focus, other writers have urged ascetical practices to render ourselves indifferent to all things. But Teilhard rejected such approaches, and has us *explicitly remember* and intensify in ourselves the concerns of those dear to us. The hopes and miseries of the earth will be the substance he will hold out to God. Their restless presence within will be the content of his prayer.

But beyond his family and friends there are unidentified others of whom he was vaguely aware; many of them can seem to be threats and recalling them leaves him troubled.

> *"I call before me the whole vast anonymous army of living humanity....This restless multitude...this ocean of humanity whose slow monotonous wave flow troubles the hearts of those whose faith is most firm: it is to this deep that I thus desire all the fibres of my being should respond."*

Beyond one's personal circle and the circle of those who share a culture with us, there are billions of humans living in radically different cultures and spread over the surface of the planet; they constitute the *"vast anonymous army of living humanity."* Teilhard would have us become aware of them and sympathize with their aspirations, but this can give us problems; this anonymous army *"troubles the hearts of those whose faith is most firm."* This problem was particularly acute for Teilhard on his first trip to China (when he wrote his "Mass on the World"). In the weeks before heading to the Ordos, he had encountered Asia as a vast and new world teeming with peoples with whom he hardly could identify. While aboard ship he noted the "swarming populations" of India and Ceylon. He quoted a lama in a novel of Kipling saying, the world is "a great and terrible thing." The lama was awed by Western civilization, but for Teilhard, "It is the immense mass of undisciplined human powers that overwhelms me."[5] On first arriving in Tientsin, he wrote in his journal: "The incoherence of Humanity = an agitated and broken sea." He soon wrote to a Jesuit friend:

> How can we hope for the spiritual and heartfelt unification of these fragments of humanity, which are spread out in every degree from savage customs to forms of new-civilization tolerably at odds with our Christian perspectives?—Cost what it will, I believe, one must hold one's self to the faith *in a direction* and in a term (even natural) of the human agitation, since, without

this faith, nothing can any longer legitimate action to our reason. But, at first view, the appearances are contrary, and crumbling and division presently seem to dominate the history of Life.[6]

This was the "Temptation of the Multiple," that is, the temptation to give up trying to make sense of human aspirations. To what did those in radically different cultures aspire? What Teilhard saw troubled his spirit and he had "to keep a tight hold on this faith [faith that all people are seeking unity], you know, when one is in the midst of the incredible diversity of man's races and preoccupations....To tell the truth, I'd find it very difficult to say what exactly goes on in the heads of people around the Pacific."[7] He has been listening with the Third Ear and he could not hear in the Chinese people any interest in mysticism or desire to unite with a single Soul. So he wrote of losing his "moral foothold."[8]

Teilhard had seen the crowded streets of Hong Kong and Peking before setting out by mule into Mongolia, where the caravan passed landscapes washed out by erosion and long lines of homeless peoples caught in the battles of conflicting warlords. He was shaken within. The people of China had become part of his world; they were a restless multitude *the immensity of which terrifies us; this ocean of humanity...troubles the hearts even of those whose faith is most firm.* He had taken on the world as his burden; humanity and its aspirations had entered his soul. They constituted the troubled world he had become and which he would hold forth in offering. If he had followed an earlier asceticism, he would have sought to make himself "indifferent." Other Jesuits had done this, but he was trying a new way to God. He was known among fellow Jesuits as one *"whose faith is most firm"*—yet, by allowing the peoples of Asia onto his paten and into his chalice, he was troubled by the *"ocean of humanity"* who seemed to lack all mystical aspiration.

"All the things in the world to which this day will bring increase; all those that will diminish; all those too that will

*die: all of them, Lord, I try to gather into my arms and hold
them out in sacrifice."*

Here Teilhard speaks of *"all the things,"* and things are easier
to deal with than people. To regain his calm, Teilhard needed time
by himself and he found this in the desert. In the desert wastes he
reestablished his peace—he called the desert his "great friend."[9]
There he could focus on and recall the divine Presence: "When I
am immersed in rocks and fossils, I sometimes feel an indefinable
bliss when I remember that I possess...the supreme Principle in
which all subsists and comes to life."[10] It was easy to see "things"
coming together in a scientific understanding, but difficult to see
how the cultures and peoples of the world could ever unite.
Inanimate things seemed to respond to the World Soul more than
the *peoples* of Asia. Eventually he would speak with a longtime missionary who assured him there was a mystical hunger in the
Chinese and showed him how he might be aware of it. For him
this was an important assurance. As the years went on Teilhard
came to know many Chinese well (most of whom were members
of the scientific community or who had been educated in the
West), and concluded they too were seeking a universal unity. On
a later trip to Asia he was no longer shaken by what he saw, and
soon came to regard Peking as his home.

> *"Yet in the very depths of this formless mass you have
> implanted...a desire, irresistible, hallowing, which makes us
> cry out, believer and unbeliever alike, 'Lord, make us one.'"*

Newly aware of the vastness of the world and the millions of
unbelievers with their customs and cultures, Teilhard saw them as
a formless mass with a disordered range of hungers. In the desert
he more or less regained his composure. There he believed, or
tried to believe, that beneath the clamor of voices and the disordered hungers, believers and unbelievers were calling for the same
thing, *"Lord, make us one."* To be *one,* that is the fundamental mystical hunger. In his first essay, "Cosmic Life," he told of seeking
unity by trying to dissolve into the universe (becoming one with

it); then with his reversal he sought a different kind of unity: all things united in a single Soul. These were two ways of responding to the hunger he believed was universal. So, for Teilhard, the individual as individual cannot be religious; only the totality of thought on earth can give rise to religion.[11] The totality of humanity, *"believer and unbeliever alike,"* is calling with a single desire, *"Lord, make us one."* It is far vaster than his "personal" desire; it is a desire as vast as the universe, yet it is in him, in him without being him *(in nobis sine nobis)*. As indicated above, there are some Christian spiritualities that call for "desirelessness"; in contrast, Teilhard wanted to receive and know in himself all the hungers/desires of humanity. Though humanity seemed to be a formless ocean of aspirations, Teilhard held to his faith that God had planted a single and hallowing desire in all peoples: the desire for a great communion. At times holding to this faith involved an uncertainty that distressed him, but at other times the common cry he "heard" reinforced his own. In terms of a more familiar psychology, at times his unconscious was joining his conscious mind with a single desire—and at times it was not.

"By that priesthood which you alone (as I firmly believe) have bestowed upon me."

In both "The Priest" and "The Mass on the World," it is clear that Teilhard is referring to his own sacramental priesthood. Yet immediately after finishing "The Priest," he wrote another essay that presents a way of Christian prayer closely resembling the prayer of "The Priest," but in the latter essay the process would apply to any Christian. An essay in the following year suggests that all Christians have "a sacred, priestly vocation."[12] As time passed, this became more explicit. In 1929 he claimed we are beginning to see the scientist and serious student as "a sort of priest, for "every work of discovery in the service of Christ, which thus hastens the growth of his mystical body, shares in his universal priesthood."[13] Later he claimed the one doing research "partakes in a very real sense of the priestly functions," and every such undertaking acquires "the sacred value of a communion."[14]

Toward the end of his life, this understanding continued: "'Scientists *[savants]* are priests."[15] And he extended this to claim "everything...becomes the business for consecration—the business of the priesthood"; he called for a new understanding of the priesthood and spoke of a "lay quasi-priest *[quasi pretre laic]*."[16] He acknowledged that in the present Church the word *priest* is reserved for those who consecrate the world in the last and supreme degree, but he wanted laypeople to understand "the degree to which they are true priests" and they too could offer his spiritual Mass.[17] When pressed for a scriptural basis for a lay priesthood, he quoted, "I come not to destroy, but to fulfil." It seems he was not then mindful of 1 Peter 2:5, where Christians form "a holy priesthood," or Revelation 1:6; 5:10; 20:6, where Christians form "a kingdom of priests" (yet in his 1940 retreat notes he refers to a passage in Revelation that speaks of Christians forming a kingdom of priests). In any case, he came to see that the sequence of prayer in his spiritual Mass (offertory, consecration, and communion) as basic to Christian prayer, and this meant all Christians are priests of a sort. That is, each Christian is called to take her or his place at the altar of the world and there offer to God the growth and diminishments of the day. Then, in faith that person accepts that God receives the offering by claiming it as Christ's body and blood (consecration). When God is seen present everywhere, one's whole life becomes a communion.

Apart from the sacramental priesthood Teilhard gave priority to the research scientist. This is because the scientist (or scholar) contributes to a common human understanding and will constitute the "supreme act of collective vision"[18] that Christ will assume.

> *"We cling so tenaciously to the illusion that fire comes forth from the depths of the earth....this idea is false....In the beginning was Power, intelligent, loving, energizing. In the beginning was the Word."*

When one looks at the fossil record a first impression would indicate that the earth spontaneously gave rise to life and its developments, yet Teilhard rejects this impression as an "illusion."

Life came from God on high. *"In the beginning was the Word,"* and this Word descended to begin creation by breathing a first trace of unity into the formless masses. Thus, "the world is not self-fecundated, but Omega fecundated."[19] The divine Word has been continuing that labor through the ages, bringing about ever larger unities. The illusion to be rejected is the claim that matter gave rise to life without any higher intervention. For Teilhard the great Source of life is to be found in God and not in matter. God is the Soul that draws all things to itself. In letting go of the contrary illusion he again tells of his reversal: the great Reality is not found in matter, it is found in the higher Soul coming to animate all things. Teilhard does not want all things to fuse together in *"the destructive fusion of which all the pantheists dream,"* but to unite (and differentiate themselves) under the influence of a single Soul. So he asks God to breathe from on high *"a soul into the newly formed, fragile film of matter with which this day the world is to be freshly clothed."* Without this higher Soul, all things would totter and crumble.

> *"Over every living thing which is to spring up, to grow, to flower, to ripen during this day say again the words: This is my Body."*

In the early morning as the earth awakens to resume its growth, the priest says, *"This is my Body."* The voices of earth have cried out for a unity they cannot give themselves. It takes the voice of God speaking through the priest, to say, "This is my Body."*** With these words *body* and *soul* earth and the divine Word come together to form the body of Christ. By repeating

---

*** The English translation of Teilhard's "The Priest" has two major mistranslations: at the consecration it has, "Let creation repeat to itself..., 'This is my Body.'" It should be "Let it [the Voice of God] repeat." This error misses a central theme of Teilhard's "The Priest": creation cannot achieve deliverance on its own; it is saved only by God's action in claiming it. The other mistranslation (which is more evident), "Master, it remains true that we are the foundation necessary to your existence." It should read, "the foundation necessary to your extension." That is, it is only by our free act of faith that God extends into our world.

Christ's words over the newly forming world, the new world is given a Soul. But the body of Christ being formed is both troubled and mortal.

> *"And over every death force which waits in readiness to corrode, to wither, to cut down, speak again your commanding words which express the supreme mystery of faith: 'This is my Blood.'"*

For Teilhard, the *"supreme* mystery of faith" refers to the second consecration, the blood. At the time he wrote his "Mass," the text of the second consecration read, *"Hic est calix sanguinis mei, novi et aeterni testamenti, mysterium fidei qui pro vobis et pro multis effundetur in remissionem peccatorum."* Here "mystery of faith" refers only to the consecration of the wine and not to the double consecration as found in the present liturgy. Seeing human growth forming the body of Christ brings us a natural satisfaction, as it goes along with our hopes; but when failure and illness limit us or when we see those we love being struck down and failing before our eyes, it is a different matter. To believe such events are also the touch of God's providence is the *"supreme mystery of faith."* We would gladly work with Christ in building a better world and ending human suffering, yet things go terribly wrong. Then we and those we love must make up in our bodies what is lacking in the passion of Christ (see Col 1:24). And slowly we come to understand that Christian salvation involves us in diminishment and death. These too can be consecrated, for Christ claims them as his blood.

What a difference it makes if we can regard our suffering and even our death as Jesus coming to meet us. St. Paul wrote, "In my flesh I complete what is lacking in Christ's afflictions." For Teilhard, that means Christ assumes my afflictions and makes them his blood. Teilhard's sister was a founder and director of the Catholic League of the Sick, a group that encouraged those suffering to offer their sufferings and limitations to God. By her prayer, Teilhard saw her "transforming into light the world's most grievous shadows." He tried to see his own disappointments in the same way and thereby avoid all bitterness. To accept failures and limitations as the touch of Christ is the supreme mystery of faith. On many occasions when friends died, he wrote letters of condolence to their families. And he often used a phrase that was important to him: "Whatever happens is adorable."[20] It is adorable as it is Christ coming for his own. In World War I, a younger Jesuit whom Teilhard knew suffered leg wounds that required amputation of both legs.[21] Teilhard wrote to him the following day: "The true comfort, is it not? (and that which keeps you light hearted, I am sure) is the thought that Our Lord himself, in his love, preferred you to be that way. And thanks to Him the deep hopes of your life are intact, and even enlarged."[22] The present author spoke with this Jesuit in October 1976; he told of the letter bringing him much comfort and reading it many times; he showed himself a happy spirit! No bitterness. Such tragedies are to be received as acts of God's loving providence. To receive them this way involves the supreme mystery of faith. So Teilhard referred to his own nervous anxieties as "another thing I must learn to adore."[23] Initially, we find such things far from adorable: "Everything is initially absurd, incoherent (chances), but all can become adorable."[24] The deaths, injuries, and anxieties of the day should be seen as adorable, for at the beginning of the day they were consecrated as the blood of Christ.

> *"Without earthquake, or thunder-clap: the flame has lit up the whole world from within. All things individually and collectively are penetrated and flooded by it....At the touch of the superstantial Word the immense host which is the universe is made flesh."*

Teilhard claimed that by our faith in Christ all things are seen to be animated by Christ. Then "things, while retaining their habitual texture, seem to be made of a different substance.... Through the operation of faith, Christ appears."[25] Here things become "*supersubstantial*" by the divine Word. There are times when things overwhelm us and we lose our "moral footing." But there are also times when all things seem to be animated by a single Soul (Supersoul) and our world lights up. We no longer see a disorganized mass, but a single life present all about us. The change is like seeing only random pixels of color on a television screen and then suddenly see them form the face of a friend. We see the same pixels of colors as before, only now they are animated as *someone*. The pixels have *"lit up...from within."* So by faith, the random pixels of life suddenly reveal a single life, that of Jesus. Faith has changed our world! *"At the touch of the supersubstantial Word the immense host which is the universe is made flesh."* Flesh is matter animated by a soul. If we believe, Christ appears as the Soul of the cosmos. Then "Everything that happens is adorable," for it is all God's doing.

On first going to Asia, Teilhard spoke of seeing the world as a veil without seam,[26] while the divine Mystery lay hidden. But, four days after returning from the expedition on which he wrote "The Mass on the World," he wrote: "My prayer should be a perpetual contemplation of the world not seen as a veil, but as Flesh." Flesh is matter animated by a soul. Soon he was writing, "My great discovery is that the world, for those who believe, becomes flesh in Christ."[27] The red earth of China "looks like wounded flesh."[28] Soon he is insisting on the world as flesh.[29] We can know we are in the divine milieu (or mystical milieu) when all things around us appear as flesh, that is, the pixels of events appear animated as the Christ. This was his "great discovery": Christians can see the world around them as the flesh of Christ, not as a concealing veil. Directly we do not see the soul (the within) of anyone, but through their flesh (gestures, hesitations, smiles, movements, voices, etc.) we come to know *them* (their souls, their withins). Likewise, when the world lights up as if animated by a Soul, matter appears as flesh, and thereby we know Christ as the Soul within all things. So Teilhard would speak of being lost *"in the mystery of the flesh of God."*[30] He ends his "Mass," *"I can preach only the mystery of your flesh, you the soul shining forth through all that surrounds me."* This would define his apostolate.

> *"Like the Flesh, it* [the universe] *attracts by the charm which floats in the mystery of its curves and folds and in the depths of its eyes."*

The flesh of another can reveal another's soul, but the flesh itself is not (or should not be) the object of our love; the soul shines *through* the flesh. The flesh itself both reveals and conceals the soul; the universe does the same with Christ. By a chemical analysis of flesh one will never come upon the soul of another; in the same way, a chemical analysis of matter will never show us Christ. He *"eludes us when submitted to analysis."* Yet the flesh of Christ is found throughout the earth.

> *"Shatter, my God, through the daring of your revelation the childishly timid outlook that can conceive of nothing greater or more vital in the world than the pitiable perfection of our human organism. On the road to a bolder comprehension of the universe the children of this world day by day outdistance the masters of Israel."*

Teilhard knew that a number of secular people were speaking of the world as a single organism of sorts—he found this in the novels of Rudyard Kipling, H. G. Wells, and Ronald Hugh Benson (not secular), and in the peace proposals of Woodrow Wilson.[31] Later he would find this understanding in the scientific reflections of Julian Huxley; today he would find it in the "Gaia hypothesis" of James Lovelock. Such people were outdistancing "the masters of Israel" (Christian leaders). Traditionally, Christians have not seen the elements of earth forming a single organism in spite of St. Paul speaking of Christ as the one in whom all things hold together. So Teilhard asks that the words of revelation might shatter Christian timidity and enable Christians to see a global, organic unity. It is the *organic* unity he is seeking, not the unity of the monist wherein all things melt together, nor the unity of the quietist in which one does nothing, nor the unity pagans have when gathered around a tangible idol. Yet, like the monist he can lose himself in the One; like the quietist he can allow himself to be cradled in the divine arms; and like the pagans he has a God whom he can touch everywhere. But it is only when striving with all his might is overcome that he will see the face of God, as happened to Jacob. *Jacob*, here and elsewhere, is a reference to Genesis 32, which tells of Jacob wrestling with an unnamed figure. After wrestling all night the figure changes Jacob's name to Israel (one who wrestles with God), "For you have striven with God and with men and have prevailed." For Teilhard it is only in our striving that we can see the face of God, as did Jacob (see Gen 32:30; Teilhard often appealed to this Old Testament passage[32]). If we remain passive, the world will hardly light up. He illustrates this by an analogy. "As on certain nights the sea around a swimmer will grow luminous, and its eddies will glisten the more brightly under the sturdy threshing of his limbs, so the dark power wrestling with the man was lit up with a thousand sparkling lights under the impact of his onslaught."[33]

> *"Each of us is our own little microcosm in which the Incarnation is wrought independently and with degrees of intensity."*

In speaking of everyone as a little microcosm, Teilhard again shows his individualism. A similar "individualism" can be seen in the old words of the Latin Mass and two of the four canons common today: *"Ut* nobis *Corpus et Sanguis fiat Domini nostri Jesu Christi."* The *nobis* suggests it will not be the body and blood of Christ for everyone, just "for us" who believe. Accordingly, Teilhard claims the divine presence is there in proportion to one's faith. *"If I firmly believe that everything around me is the body and blood of the Word, then for me (and in one sense for me alone) is brought about that marvelous 'diaphany' which causes the luminous warmth of a single life to be objectively discernable in and to shine forth from the depths of every event, every element."* Teilhard often referred to the diaphany of creatures and preferred "diaphany" to "epiphany."[34] Diaphany is a Greek term telling of something revealed *through* (the world) as opposed to epiphany, which tells of something revealed *in* the world. Teilhard's point can be understood in the way we know a friend. We can see only the friend's physical body, but by observing the physical we sometimes "intuit" the soul shining *through* the visible smiles and gestures. We could say the soul was shining "in" the gestures, but Teilhard preferred diaphany;

perhaps his choice of words also suggests that God remains radically transcendent. On the feast of the Epiphany he prayed, "Master, grant me the diaphany."[35]

Teilhard recognized that many lovers seek unity almost exclusively in the physical. But he believed unity is not to be found there (such lovers have not made their reversal!); in seeking only a physical union these lovers will find themselves increasingly alienated from one another. Bodies can press together but they cannot unite; only the souls of lovers can unite in a higher Soul, Christ, the World Soul. (He explained this to the important women in his life.) At the same time, to relate to others more than pure spirits are needed. Spirits must express themselves *through* the physical—but the physical is not the object one loves. Again, Teilhard is seeking diaphany, spirit showing through the matter.

On occasions the monotony of things "lights up" and one can intuit the divine Soul animating everything. A "deep brilliance" is seen at the heart of everything.[36] Things seem more deeply themselves and at the same time one with all else; "union [things are one] differentiates [they are more deeply themselves]." Some people claim we know of God by witnessing miracles or by accepting that miracles happened on the testimony of others. But, for Teilhard, God rarely intervenes in the course of world events; rather, "God [is] uniquely a vision of the 'within' of things."[37] Then the world is seen as flesh; the universe shows its "within," its Soul. To have this "vision," Teilhard claims we need faith, so he prays, *"Lord,…that in every creature I may discover and sense you, I beg you: give me faith."*

> *"What I must do, when I have taken part with all my energies in the consecration which causes its flames to leap forth, is to consent to the communion which will enable it to find in me the food it has come in the last resort to seek."*

Teilhard offers his "Mass" at the first light of dawn; soon he will be taken up with the events of the day, and these events will constitute the communion of his "Mass." His faith has enabled him to see Christ as Soul of the World, but he must pass beyond seeing to the day's work. But his universal vision enables him to have a universal communion. "Faith consecrates the world. Fidelity communicates with it."[38] The time comes when he must "communicate through fidelity with the world as consecrated by faith." In his retreat notes for 1946 he wrote "consecration = Faith / communion = Fidelity."[39] Faith enables us to contemplate a consecrated world, and, with fidelity to the vision, every event of our life can be a moment of communion.

The coming day will carry us beyond what we intend, yet Teilhard reaches out toward the day's events, the fiery bread set before him. He knows events will tear him from himself and drive him into labors, danger, a renewal of ideas, and an austere detachment of his affections. Such is the life of anyone who tries to live for an ideal. By life itself he will acquire a hunger for things beyond life and beyond all he can identify. He will consume the Host, but the greater truth is that the Host will consume him. The Host will *"find in me the food it has come in the last resort to seek."* He quotes St. Gregory of Nyssa, "It is the bread that assimilates us, and not we the bread, when we receive it." A similar thought is found in St. Augustine, who spoke of the "devouring power" of the Eucharist.[40]

> *"It is a terrible thing to have been born: I mean, to find oneself, without having willed it, swept irrevocable along on a torrent of fearful energy which seems as though it wished to destroy everything it carries with it. What I want, my God, by a reversal of forces which you alone can bring about, my terror in face of the nameless changes destined to renew my being may be turned into an overflowing joy at being transformed into you."*

Here, for the second time in his "Mass," Teilhard tells of his reversal. In seeing only the scientific picture, one can believe that the millions of living beings have simply arisen from the earth, and the energy that has brought things to life *"seems as though it wished to destroy"* all it has created. To reject this position, Teilhard offers a personal testimony: "For a Christian working in the field of research, scientific activities take on marvelous significance once he *reverses* the mechanistic point of view and places the principle of movement, which the nineteenth century believed it had discovered at the antipodes to God, in an upper Pole of creative action."[41] When Teilhard first told of the reversal in "Cosmic Life," he offered no explanation. Here, twenty-some years later, he gives personal testimony of the "marvelous significance" he found by making the reversal. Prayer had played a part.[42]

Teilhard speaks here of the changes *"destined"* to renew his being. His individual destiny was part of a wider destiny, for all things are *"destined* to be completed in the future."[43] He called his going to China "the decisive moment of my destiny."[44] For Teilhard, destiny was not an impersonal force, but the action of Christ, the loving Soul of the World. So in getting his doctorate, he reflected, "All takes place before me and within me with a 'palpable solicitude' of events."[45] While writing his "Mass," he believed God was tending to him personally: "For the last two months we could not go where we wanted, and found something [of scientific interest] everywhere. I believe the Lord leads us."[46] And later, "It seems to me that Our Lord has really led me by the hand these last three months."[47] In 1929, he believed it was "perhaps more than chance" that arranged his presence in the lab in Peking when the first skull of Peking Man was brought there; this left him "enamoured of the divine influence that controls the world.[48] Arriving in Java right after a significant discovery was made (a child's skull known as the "Mojokerto Child"—now dated as 1.8 million years old!), he asked, "What did they mean, these successive strokes of good luck. What is God requesting of me?"[49] He did not see an impersonal fate; he wrote to a non-Christian friend: "May Life become for you not just some blind, favorable fatality, but a kind of living Presence or Benevolence in which it will be possible for you not only to trust, but to confide."[50]

This benevolent and personal Destiny was protecting evolution. This is evident even in *The Phenomenon of Man*, a work he considered a "scientific memoire." But a fundamental line of his argument goes beyond science to claim Providence has been taking a direct and personal care of the planet: "To bring us into existence it [the world] has juggled miraculously with too many improbabilities for there to be any risk whatever in following it right to the end." Some might imagine the earth ending in disasters (comets striking the earth, etc.), but "however possible they may be in theory, we have higher reasons for being sure *that they will not happen.*"[51] The higher reasons come from his faith that Christ will bring his body to completion. He even tells of "a secret complicity between the infinite and the infinitesimal to warm, nourish and sustain" us.[52] Such phrases imply a personal Providence leading him and the world to their consummation. So in the Mass the destiny he will receive that day comes from a personal God who has selected it for him, and the Eucharist contains *"the secret of that destiny you have chosen for me."* But to achieve his destiny, he must freely reach out to accept the Host, not knowing what it will bring.

> *"First of all I stretch out my hand unhesitatingly towards the fiery bread which you set before me....The man who is filled with an impassioned love of Jesus hidden in the forces which bring increase to the earth, him the earth will lift up, like a mother in the immensity of her arms, and will enable him to contemplate the face of God."*

Teilhard must follow the principle that has worked for him in the past: "Let nothing be untried. It will be a bad sign if I find I am traveling on level ground and not engaged in a venture that costs me."[53] At his morning Mass (during his lifetime, all Masses were in the morning) he knows the day will involve him in a whirlpool of activity; he will be driven into danger, labor, and a constant renewal of ideas. Yet, if he continually reaches for new challenges, he will gain a taste for God in everything and above everything—a taste that will estrange him from the ordinary joys that others know. But the forces that bring increase to the earth will lift him up, as a mother lifts her child, and will *"enable him to contemplate the face of God."* Note: the earth does not oppose God; it raises Teilhard to God. The gaze of faith sees the world aglow as Christ, the face of God, a glow that is brighter when one is actively engaged. St. Ignatius was described by an associate as a "contemplative in action," and for Teilhard it is especially in action that we are able to see God, to contemplate; he had difficulty with quieter forms of prayer, and found God more in activities. "Action becomes contemplation….Action…is the milieu of union."[54]

But seeing is not the same as union. For seeing itself implies a duality, a separation between the seer and the object seen. To attain union, he must step beyond seeing—he can proceed only by faith. It will involve a radical diminishment. For in seeking *"union with a pre-existent Being,"* one of the two must die.

> *"If my being is ever to be definitively attached to yours, there must first die in me not merely the monad ego but also the world: in other words I must first pass through an agonizing phase of diminution for which no tangible compensation will be given me. That is why, pouring into my chalice the bitterness of all separations, of all sterile fallings away, you hold it out to me. 'Drink ye all of this.'"*

Teilhard first developed his ideas on the Mass while active in what was the most destructive war in history, but the war heightened his sense of life.[55] Life seemed more precious than ever, yet he was ready to abandon it without regret. "We must have a great love for the world if we are passionately to wish to leave it behind."[56] In war, life and death come together, as they do in communion (the body and the blood). Having taken his fill of the universe, he was possessed by a need to die and leave it behind. Receiving the Host has made him long for the next phase of the one sacrament: he must drink from the chalice. By receiving the bread *"there has crept into the marrow of my being an inextinguishable longing to be united with you beyond life; through death."*

If he were to refuse the chalice, his communion would not be Christian. Now he must accept the dark side of the coming day, the failures, the aging, the frustrations, the forces that will eventually consume him and the universe. Here Teilhard joins the long and familiar Christian tradition of renouncing the world. But for

Teilhard this should occur only within a life fully lived (the first part of his communion). Each day he will be given the chalice, and each day his communion with the blood of Christ will continue. But this communion will be complete only in death.

He prays, *"There must first die in me, not merely the monad ego, but also the world."* Note, the world that must die is *his* world (the world *"in me"*). "The supreme salvific transformation of the universe consists in its conscious 'annihilation' in God." And "Christ, in the cosmos, is the Center of union in annihilation."[57] The second phase of his communion will be complete only with his death.

All faithful Christians pray to receive communion at the hour of death, but Teilhard asks for something more: "Teach me to treat my death as an act of communion."[58] "When I die, my strength will be, I sense it, to let myself slide into the Heart of the World."[59] Heart of the World! His body and even his mind will disintegrate into the earth. But Teilhard believed Jesus gave his heart to the world. And there he can be found: Jesus *in the forces that bring death to the earth.* "To find Him…What a thrill."[60]

> *"The man who is filled with an impassioned love for Jesus hidden in the forces which bring death to the earth, him the earth will clasp in the immensity of her arms as her strength fails, and with her he will awaken in the bosom of God."*

In receiving the Host Teilhard was raised to "contemplate the face of God," but still he and God were apart as the seer is apart from the object seen. Now in drinking from the chalice he will be taken into the divine bosom where there is no distance between God and himself, where all seeing is ended: so drinking from the chalice is the supreme mystery of faith. To enter into God, there must be a "rupture" on the part of God as he admits creatures into himself, and a rupture on the part of creatures to enter.[61] The rupture requires a complete break with the natural order; it is our communion with the death of Christ. Teilhard has told of two phases in life, development and diminishment, and the latter is complete with death. By one's life a victim is being prepared— one's self; as the Mass continues the victim is sacrificed, for fundamentally the Mass is a sacrifice (John Paul II: "The Eucharist is a sacrifice in the strict sense"[62]). In any Mass, Christ is both the priest and the victim. And, in the great Mass that constitutes our life, each believer is the same, the priest and the victim. And on the altar of the world each priest will be sacrificed. But if one lives by faith, he will believe "he is being driven out of himself and that he is dying, under the compelling power of a Communion."[63]

Only in drinking the chalice to the bitter end does one enter the divine bosom. Only by an "annihilation," passing through a zero point, can one's communion be complete. Teilhard and his world, like Christ and his world dying on the cross, must pass through a total night, and then *"as her* [his world's] *strength fails, he will awaken with her in the bosom of God."* The world he loved has passed with him through the night, the zero point. He and his world attain salvation only beyond the annihilation of everything that looks like an advance for himself and humanity. In the end, no worldly compensation will be given, for there can be none. In building his body we more or less *see* things light up with Christ (Teilhard's essays often would teach us to see), but, in drinking from the chalice, there is no seeing, no visible assurance. While writing his "Mass" he wrote to a friend: *"Beati sunt qui non viderunt et crediderunt* [Blessed are those who do not see and yet believe]."[64] Teilhard spoke of himself as a "seer" and identified many of his writings as efforts to see Christ everywhere. But he also points to the chalice that takes us beyond everything. It is only beyond all phenomena that God saves us and our world.[65] We and our world must pass through a dark night before we can enter a new heaven and a new earth. The dark night is our communion with the blood of Christ.

> *"Lord, lock me up in the deepest depths of your heart. And then, holding me there, burn me, purify me, set me on fire, sublimate me till I become utterly what you would have me be, through the utter annihilation of my ego."*

Teilhard identifies this as the prayer of a sixteenth-century Jesuit, calling it "a little strong, but most beautiful," but neither the present author, nor Henri de Lubac, nor others have been able to identify the author.[66] Here Teilhard agrees with the long Christian ascetical tradition that spoke of a dark night of the senses and a dark night of the soul. (He differed only in insisting one must begin with a natural growth: "The fruit must be ripe before it can split and open.") "We need alternately the work that widens our being and the sorrow that brings death to it, the life that makes a man greater in order that he may be sanctifiable and the death that makes him less in order that he may be sanctified."[67] He would tell abundantly of a growth followed by a diminishment and even tell of preferring the latter. "To center, individualize and personalize oneself is half the joy of life, the other and better half being, as we shall repeat, is to de-center oneself in a Being greater than oneself."[68] For, in the end, only the de-centering of death enables one to end the duality of subject-seeing-object-seen, and, thereby, enter the divine Bosom.

> *"As long as I could see—or dared to see—in you, Lord Jesus, only the man who lived two thousand years ago, the sublime moral teacher, the Friend, the Brother, my love remained timid and constrained...and never before was there anyone before whom I could in honesty bow down."*

It is only in seeing Christ shining within all things that Christ could be seen as Lord of the world, and this made a difference in the way Teilhard could pray. In some forms of prayer we speak to Jesus as teacher, friend, and brother—a true form of prayer—but there is also adoration. Adoration is a complete form of prayer, and Teilhard claims that as humanity becomes more and more conscious, it will feel more and more the need to adore.

To adore...That means to lose oneself in the unfathomable, to plunge into the inexhaustible, to find peace in the incorruptible, to be absorbed in defined immensity, to offer oneself to the fire and the transparency, to annihilate oneself in proportion as one becomes more deliberately conscious of oneself, and to give of one's deepest to that whose depth has no end.[69]

When Christ is seen as the world Soul, he is seen as unifying everything in himself. He is no longer simply teacher and friend, for now his forehead is of the whiteness of snow, his eyes are of fire, and his feet are brighter than molten gold. Only then is he known as one's Lord and God.

> *"When two centuries ago, your Church began to feel the particular power of your heart, it might have seemed that what was captivating men's souls was the fact of their finding in you an element even more determinate, more circumscribed, than your humanity as a whole."*

Teilhard is referring to devotion to the Sacred Heart. Here he speaks of the devotion having a particular power "two centuries ago"; elsewhere he tells how the devotion "in the France of Louis XIV [+1715] assumed an astonishing vigorous form."[70] The devotion seems to have begun in the early Middle Ages. It was preached by Benedictines and Franciscans and later became an important element in Jesuit devotion. It became widely popular following the visions of St. Margaret Mary Alacoque (1747–96). Teilhard says his mother "constantly sustained" him by the devotion and it played a "central, seminal part" in his life.[71] In his spiritual autobiography, he tells of gazing at a picture of the Sacred Heart (an incident difficult to date, but probably shortly before he left Egypt in 1908[72]): "I saw a mysterious patch of crimson and gold delineated in the very centre of the Saviour's breast, I found what I was looking for": the whole reality of the cosmic Christ seemed visibly condensed into a compact object, Christ as the Christic and freed from all "restrictive particularity";[73] that is, Christ without a particular face.

During the war, Teilhard wrote an imaginative account of a priest having a vision while praying before a picture of "Christ with his Heart offered to men." The outline of Christ's face and his robes seemed to spread outward into the world so that the uni-

Picture of the Sacred Heart
that Teilhard carried with him for most of his life

verse was vibrating: "All this movement seemed to emanate from Christ—from his Heart in particular."[74] In telling of the devotion being "central and seminal" to his thought, Teilhard is telling above all of the moment when the scientific movement to greater complexity took on the heart and face he knew in his Christian devotions. For much of his life he carried with him a small "holy card" showing Christ offering his heart to the world. He gave this card to Lucile Swan as she was leaving China in 1941; later he got another copy of the same card, which was standing on his writing table when he died.

> *"Glorious Lord Christ,…you who are the first and the last, the living and the dead and the risen again; you who gather into your exuberant unity every beauty, every affinity, every energy, every mode of existence; it is you to whom my being cried out with a desire as vast as the universe, 'In truth you are my Lord and my God.'"*

In the offertory, Teilhard recalled all the elements that made up his world *("one by one, Lord...")*, and then heard these elements expressing within him an enormous desire, *"Lord, make us one."* The consecration followed wherein the Lord responded to the desire of earth by claiming the world as his body uniting all things in a common Soul. This Soul shines through the body (the universe) as our souls shine through our bodies (in seeing our body people understand our soul), and at that moment the universe is in adoration; the desires of the world are attaining what they sought, their unifying Soul. So the spirituality of Teilhard leads to the satisfaction of desire, as opposed to the spiritualities that eliminate it: "The Buddhist denies himself to kill desire (he does not believe in the value of being). While the authentic Christian makes the same gesture by an excess of desire and of faith in the value of being."[75] In the "Mass," Teilhard's desire has become *"as vast as the universe,"* and can be satisfied only in the Lord of the universe. We can be unaware of God because our desires are too small, but when all that is within us has become a cry for unity, we become aware of a need to adore. Then we are loving God "with every fibre of the unifying universe," "with the whole universe."[76] With our limited personal desires we can speak with Jesus as teacher and friend, but adoration involves all that is *"in nobis sine nobis,"* "within us without being us." Our world is at prayer: "Sun and moon, bless the Lord." In adoration, that is what the sun and the moon are doing.

Teilhard spoke of the world within somewhat as others speak of the unconscious or subconscious. Using such terms, the conscious mind can talk with Jesus as teacher or friend, while the unconscious is only marginally involved. In adoration the conscious and unconscious minds act together. Then *we* (that is, our conscious minds) speak with *"a desire as vast as the universe"* (the elements that constitute our unconscious minds); we speak with all that is *in nobis, sine nobis*. Such moments come to us as a "grace."

> *"This is the criterion by which I can judge at each moment how far I have progressed within you. When all things*

around me, while preserving their own individual contours, their own special savours, nevertheless appear to me as animated by a single secret spirit."

This is again "union differentiates." One knows a unity *("a single...spirit")* that differentiates *("preserving their own individual contours").* Now in the course of the day, the ongoing differentiation of events assures him that Teilhard is following the will of God, that he is living in the divine milieu. Should things no longer appear to be animated by a single life, should events no longer appear as flesh, he will know he has taken a wrong step. And, if life becomes an undefined blur (differentiation is lacking), again, he has taken a wrong step. That is how a scientist proceeds with his or her hypothesis and the way the believer should proceed with faith. When a friend suggested that Teilhard leave the Church and be free to publish, he replied, "If I leave the Church, the Immense Beauty that attracts me will disappear as inconsistent smoke."[77] When it was pointed out that he could leave the Jesuits, remain a priest, and publish, he replied, "I would thus leave my divine Milieu. It is in the Society that the grace of God awaits me."[78] For within the Society he lived "under the impression of a continual communion."[79] Where there is life, there is the union that differentiates. His first essay ("Cosmic Life") told of taking the direction of increasing life as opposed to the direction of dissolution: "I now have a deep conviction, dear to me, infinitely precious and unshakable, the humblest and yet the most fundamental in the whole structure of my convictions, that life is never mistaken, either about its road or its destination."[80] Where there is life, there is a unity increasingly differentiating everything around us; that is, when we see this way, we are living in the divine milieu.

"Fill my heart alternately with exaltation and with distaste."

The mystic longs for what is beyond this world. Yet Teilhard believed the mystic will first try to be like others, "to see as they do, to speak their language, to find his contentment in the joys with which they are satisfied."[81] But they are not enough, so the mystic might turn to art or literature, but the time will come when these too show their inadequacy. Then the mystic begins to long for what is beyond exaltation and distaste. In addressing the "Glorious Lord Christ" Teilhard spoke to Christ as *the living the dead and the risen again.*" In his ongoing search each element lights up and then darkens, and he turns from each with distaste. Finally he comes to a moment of annihilation wherein he unites with the dying Lord. Teilhard is saying we must first know God's presence in all things *("the living")* and then his absence in all things *("the dead")*; only then do we become aware of the God beyond all things *("the risen again")*.

In the meantime, things of the world will show him their sweetness and their malice, their power and their weakness; he will know both exaltation and distaste. But these dual elements are only the gently alternating phases (body then blood) of a single communion.

> *"It is to your body in this its fullest extension...that I dedicate myself...with the all too feeble resources of my scientific knowledge, with my religious vows, with my priesthood, and (most dear to me) with my deepest human convictions. It is in this dedication, Lord Jesus, I desire to live, in this I desire to die."*

On May 26, 1918, while on military furlough in Paris, Teilhard took solemn vows of poverty, chastity, and obedience as a Jesuit. He told of not having a moment's misgiving: "I placed my trust in God."[82] Soon after vows he wrote "The Priest," ending it with what seems like a further vow: "To bring Christ by virtue of a specific organic connection, to the heart of realities that are esteemed the most dangerous, the most unspiritual, the most pagan—in that you have my Gospel and my mission."[83] Here and elsewhere he speaks of "my Gospel."[84] This "Gospel" concerned the flesh of Christ, what he had been given to preach. Preaching this involved venturing into the unknown where the vision by which he lived would be threatened. This would cause distress, but he had faith that the strange and unfamiliar worlds that troubled him would eventually be seen as Christ. Yet when he first entered such worlds he was shaken and confused. He tells of going to Somalia and Abyssinia "guided by that general principle of my life to never let pass any occasion to experiment and search."[85] That is, he would always reach for *"the fiery bread."*

His "Mass on the World" ends with a brief dedication that *"springs from the inmost fibres of [his] being."* In 1951 he considered writing another version of his "Mass" and there he wanted to reaffirm his dedication: "In all of my weakness, with all my age, with all my passion [I wish] to revow myself to the Revelation of the Universal Heart of Christ."[86]

Notes

1. LT, 86.
2. Ex 28; Wis 18:24; Ringgren, 9, 13.
3. Barbour, 23; Cuenot, 85.
4. F, 17.
5. LT, 70.
6. Li, 104.
7. LLZ, 48.
8. Lukas, 77.
9. LGI, 45; LTF, 38.
10. LLZ, 72.
11. C, 119.
12. HM, 217.
13. T, 16.
14. HE, 179.
15. LMF, 149.
16. LMF, 196.
17. LMF, 196–97.
18. P, 249.
19. Nr, 190.

20. LT, 183, 288, 144; Li, 350; Barbour, 147; UL, Arsenne, November 24, 1943; UL, Breuil, September 23, 1947.
21. MM, 100.
22. UL, De Greusser, April 8, 1916.
23. Barbour, 148.
24. J, April 11, 1952.
25. W, 246.
26. LT, 70.
27. UJ, November 14, 1923.
28. LT, 98.
29. S, 75, 76, 77.
30. HM, 126.
31. MM, 271–78; HM, 213.
32. HM, 69; HE, 181; J, 37, 40, 50; LGI, 72; Nr, 73; see D, 108, 112.
33. HM, 70.
34. LLZ, 74.
35. J, January 6, 1925.
36. D, 130.
37. J, November 7, 1923.
38. D, 138.
39. LLZ, 66; Nr, 276.
40. S, 76; W, 210.
41. HE, 179.
42. LJM, 10.
43. W, 169; emphasis added.
44. HM, 153; translation amended.
45. J, March 23, 1922.
46. UL, July 25, 1923.
47. LT, 88.
48. Li, 204; Cuenot, 97.
49. Speight, 222; for fossil date, see Swisher, 83, 84.
50. LTF, 33.
51. P, 233, 275; italics in text.
52. P, 267, 276; see also HM, 74.
53. J, March 23, 1922.
54. J, December 21, 1923.
55. LGI, 46.

56. HM, 174; W, 262.
57. Nr, 65, 67.
58. D, 90.
59. J, October 8, 1923.
60. Nr, 223.
61. LLZ, 95.
62. Or, 757.
63. W, 261.
64. LT, 88.
65. See D, 60.
66. MM, 203; see Cor, 88.
67. W, 209.
68. HE, 30.
69. D, 128.
70. HM, 43; T, 98, 99.
71. HM, 42.
72. HM, 44.
73. HM, 43.
74. HM, 63
75. Li, 246; parentheses in text.
76. P, 297; HE, 159.
77. J, June, 28, 1925.
78. LJM, 27.
79. UL, Gaudefroy, November 12, 1926.
80. W, 32; italics in text.
81. W, 119.
82. Cuenot, 27.
83. W, 220.
84. Nr, 114; J, 70, 71.
85. Li, 181.
86. October 8, 1951.

6.

THE "MASS" AND ADORATION

"In truth, you are my Lord and my God."

Near the end of his "Mass," Teilhard prayed to the risen Lord with "a desire as vast as the universe, 'In truth, you are my Lord and my God.'" By praying with such a desire his prayer has become adoration. The final words, "My Lord and my God," pick up the words Thomas the apostle spoke to Jesus one week after his resurrection.

When Jesus first appeared to his disciples on Easter Sunday, Thomas was not there. When Thomas returned, the other apostles told of the appearance of Jesus, but Thomas refused to believe. Then a week later, Thomas was with them when the risen Lord appeared again. Jesus told Thomas to put his fingers into his wounds, saying, "Do not be faithless, but believing." Thomas exclaimed, "My Lord and my God." Jesus said, "Have you believed because you have seen me? Blessed are those who have not seen and yet believe" (John 20:29).

Jesus rebuked Thomas for his lack of faith, and since then a long tradition has called him "doubting Thomas." Yet Thomas's exclamation, "My Lord and my God," is one of the strongest statements of the divinity of Jesus in the New Testament. Thomas had known Jesus as a teacher and friend, but only in seeing/touching the risen body did he know Jesus as his Lord and God. It took a direct experience of Jesus as Lord for Thomas's prayer to become adoration—and so with Teilhard.

Jesus called "blessed" those who believe without seeing, and most Christians would identify themselves this way. Down the centuries many have accepted the resurrection on the testimony of the apostles and the faith community that followed them. Such followers could well be termed *blessed*, but Thomas was not among them. He wanted direct evidence. He took the world seriously and in doing so was unable to believe all he was told. It was only when his sight agreed with what he was told that Thomas could say, "My Lord and my God." All those who take the world seriously can experience what Thomas did, but it is just such people who can come to adoration.

In Teilhard's "Mass" shortly before quoting Thomas, he told of a limitation he once had in his knowing of Jesus: *"As long as I could see—or dared to see—in you, Lord Jesus, only the man who lived two thousand years ago, the sublime moral teacher, the Friend, the Brother, my love remained timid and constrained."* Teilhard came from a devout family and entered easily into his family's faith. But in looking back to when he was six or seven he found his "real me" was elsewhere, practicing a private devotion to his "God of Iron," bits of discarded metal that seemed indestructible.[1] Learning that iron rusts, he almost despaired: "I threw myself down on the lawn and shed the bitterest tears of my existence"; he had to look elsewhere for what would endure. Soon his attention turned to the rocks and the ultimate matter of earth—again, that which seemed indestructible, eternal.

This "instinctive" love for matter did not fit well with the family religion he was taught. So he felt pulled in two directions. In finishing *college* he decided for the religion he was taught, and shortly before his eighteenth birthday entered the Jesuit Order to begin studies for the priesthood. But his "real me" still reached out to the rocks—the world of direct experience as apart from the world of faith. His interest in the rocks caused him some difficulty as a Jesuit novice, but soon, with the encouragement of Jesuit authorities, he decided to become both a priest and a geologist. Then, after eight years as an observant Jesuit working in geology, he found himself with a "somewhat muddled spiritual complex within."[2] His religion was partly composed of faith in what loving people had told him, and "blessed" are those who can do that— but, like Thomas, Teilhard was not among them. His "real me" reached for the rocks. He felt caught *"between two absolutes."*[3] Eventually, the conflicting devotions came together in "an explosion of dazzling flashes," what Teilhard called "the great event of my life."[4] This was the moment when, looking at a picture of the Sacred Heart, he saw Christ's heart as the loving center of the universe—Christ's heart was where the absolutes had joined. After this Teilhard *believed* and *saw* a single reality. Many of his fellow Jesuits knew him as having a more profound faith than they—for most of them had come from loving families, or a faith community they trusted, and they simply believed. "Blessed are they."

In his "Mass," after describing his knowledge of Jesus as brother, teacher, and friend, he told of finding the cosmic reality of Jesus: *"Master...you shine forth from within all the forces of the earth and so become* visible *to me."* Visible! When *seeing* is added to believing, Teilhard—like Thomas—can adore. It is through our senses, our seeing, touching, and tasting, that the universe enters into us to become our spirit. And in the offertory it is this "totality of a universe that has been deposited in him"[5] that cries, "Lord make us one." As the Mass ends he finds the "totality of a universe" within calling "with a desire as vast as the universe, 'My Lord and my God.'" This is adoration: Teilhard and his universe are at prayer.

By many of his works Teilhard was teaching others to see (his first essay was "to make men see"; *The Divine Milieu* was "to teach how to see"; *The Phenomenon of Man* was an attempt "to see and make others see," and so forth.[6] Without seeing we can believe, but we will not be able to adore. The difference made him anxious in first encountering the multitudes of Asia. For he could not *see* them having any mystical interest (they did not seem to seek a single soul). So a day or two before heading into the Ordos, he noted in his journal that the one prayer necessary for him was, "That I may see." In other terms, when we are able to adore, then our conscious reflective mind believes a revelation that is consonant with what our less than conscious mind knows: a world hungry for a Soul. In adoration the two complement one another.

To better understand Teilhard's adoration consider an imaginative essay, "The Spiritual Power of Matter," written in 1919 as he was being demobilized and returning to the quiet of Jesuit life. It tells of two travelers (they could be identified as Teilhard and a fellow Jesuit) walking in a desert when Matter swoops down and becomes a hurricane within one of them (Teilhard). Matter says, "You called me: here I am. Driven by the Spirit far from humanity's caravan routes, you dared to venture into the untouched wilderness; grown weary of abstractions, of attenuations, of the wordiness of social life, you wanted to pit yourself against Reality entire and untamed."[7] The man has gone apart from "humanity's caravan routes" and "the wordiness of social life." He has left even his companion behind. In the caravan routes, people are telling one another what they believe: "Well I believe…," "In our church we say…," "Here is the revealed truth," "No, it is here." Bewildered by claims and counterclaims, the call of the desert is a call of the "real me" to set aside all one is asked to believe and see what *is*.

Apart from "humanity's caravan route," matter is a challenge and a threat. The one who meets it must struggle to survive. But by the struggle one sees "with pitiless clarity, the ridiculous pretentiousness of human claims to order the life of the world, to impose on the world the dogmas, the standards, the conventions of men"; and the traveler finds in matter a *point d'appui* "*outside* the confines of human society."[8] He has left the shelter of words and the assurances of culture (Christian or otherwise) to return to immediate experience. There in a struggle to understand, he realizes he "can never go back, never return to commonplace gratifications or untroubled worship."[9] Untroubled worship! At this point Teilhard could well say, "Blessed are they who believe without seeing." But in looking for more than simple belief, he was not one of them. His worship had become troubled, for all *seeing* is ambiguous. It was not always evident that the world was seeking a single Soul. But, in trying to see, he can no longer rejoin his faithful companion prostrate on the desert floor; henceforth, Teilhard the *seer* will be a stranger to the simple believer. He will be separated even from "his brothers in God, better men than he"—may they be blessed! "He would inevitably speak henceforth in an incomprehensible tongue, he whom the Lord had drawn to follow the road of fire."[10] The road of fire tells of the troubled path one finds in stepping apart from the community culture to wrestle with the whirlwinds of earth.

Through Teilhard's struggles (his work in science, his original philosophy, his effort to dominate his passions, etc.) he begins to see matter, that which at first seemed a blind and feral threat, become personal with an ineffable face. Matter announces it will achieve its "definitive salvation" through the words of the Mass: "This is my Body."[11] Here in the desert, the revealed word of God is claiming what Teilhard's "real me" has *seen*. This is the consecration. And, if he believes, all the fibers of the unifying universe appear centered on an adorable Someone.

Teilhard found most of those with whom he worked would say, "Religion is a personal matter." They were saying that each had, without need of or possibility of evidence, made up one's mind and that was that.[12] They were "blessed" with some sort of an answer. He compared such people to the people chatting in the reception hall of a great ship and telling each other what they believed, while he had gone out on the deck and *seen* the ship was moving; the earth was going somewhere.[13] He tried to get churchmen and scientists to open their eyes and see a strong underlying current moving humanity to a destiny to which they were blind. Churchmen and scientists had become prisoners in their differing conventions, while Teilhard was called apart from both of them, apart from the banter of "humanity's caravan route." And apart from any belief-community he had come upon a point of support by which he could *evaluate the different creeds*. He had seen the whirlwind of events light up with a single Soul, and what he saw fit well with the Christ who claimed the world as his body.

In finding a god apart from the human caravan, life became difficult for Teilhard. He would never know "untroubled worship." Years later he reflected, such a one "will at times be unable to shake off a feeling of terror. He will not be able to hold back, but he will be frightened by the novelty, the boldness and at the same time the paradoxical potentialities of attitudes that he finds himself, intellectually and emotionally, obliged to adopt."[14] Though "unable to shake off his feeling of terror," Teilhard knew he was on "a grand and glorious venture." But he added, "I still tremble often as I pursue it." He had taken on the universe as a personal burden. Why? Why does anyone do so? The universe—*le Tout*—had "summoned" him; and with the account of the call he began his literary career. Yet it seems a similar call was present as he began his life.[15] His response was a bold plunge into the current of things, and with that the universe became his burden. He set out on the road of fire and in the years that followed he would pay the price.

Many people considered bipolar have taken on the world as a burden. In a limited sense we could see Teilhard, with his mix of creativity and depression, as bipolar. But, beyond bipolarity as an illness, he knew it as two forms of grace. So his "Mass" tells of a bipolar communion: there is the body (the world-as-Christ living and Teilhard shares his life) and the blood (the world-as-Christ dying and he shares Christ's death). His faith both comforted him and troubled him, troubled him when he could not see the immanent divinity hidden in events.

Two weeks before his death, Teilhard wrote an essay, "Research, Work and Adoration." There he describes Jesuit authorities telling him on many occasions, "Go quietly ahead with your scientific work without getting involved in philosophy or theology."[16] Certainly many scientists have worked with little concern for these subjects; perhaps they simply enjoy their work or find science a means of livelihood. But Teilhard also believed many scientists, like himself, were moved by a surge of worship toward the world.[17] Through knowing the world by science (evolution, etc.), he felt adoration toward a future world that was coming to be. He believed many scientists sensed a sacred future to which they wanted to contribute; workers had the same sense. If one were a Christian, one would be confused by feelings of worship directed toward an immanent god. On the one hand, the believer wants to follow the God of whom one has been taught, while on the other hand, one knows another god through work. Believing and seeing can leave one serving two masters, loving one and despising the other—or maybe just confused.

The many writings of Teilhard attempt to bring the scientific world known from experience together with the Christian gospel received in faith. Since experience involves the "real me," there is something in us that cannot simply be told what to believe. For Teilhard, one must wrestle directly with the world (as scientist or worker), and in doing so the "real me" comes to suspect an immanent divinity up ahead. On one occasion he wrote of a "dark adoration of the God before us"—this is the adoration of the god of the nonbelieving physicists and the naturalists,[18] the god of those without Christian faith. For this dark adoration to become luminous, it needs the light of Christian revelation—a belief beyond what is seen. So Teilhard tried to show his scientific friends and those who took the world seriously how Christian faith could illumine what they were finding.

Teilhard did not see present-day Christology meeting the need of such people: "There is a crowd of Christians who no longer believe, and they no longer believe because the figure of Christ presented to them is no longer up to their faculties of adoration."[19] "Roman theologians" were holding to an understanding of Christ too small to be adored.[20] He even believed his Jesuit friend Henri de Lubac and other theologians let the revelation *blind* them to this world[21]—they continued believing, but they did not *see*. Many Christians had looked to the Church to identify the Soul they were finding *immanent* to their work, while the Church told them of a *transcendent* God and of Jesus, an ideal human being. So many were unable to recognize what they were finding. Some turned from the Church, while others accepted what they were told and set the matter aside to engage themselves with the world; perhaps they continued to find Jesus in church, but could not identify what they were finding in their work. For such people, Christian faith *did not engage their mind,* their "real me." For this to happen they needed to wrestle with the world, either to understand it through research or to take a course of action (work).

In research the mind works to unify what it is finding and in doing so senses a unifying Power far greater than its own, "the Power that organizes all."[22] Adoration is now possible. "Adoration's real name...is Research." "I see less and less difference (intellectually and psychologically) between Research and

Adoration."[23] Teilhard speaks of research as prayer and "perhaps the highest form of prayer," and without "research there can be no possibility...of real mystical life."[24] Those with minds engaged in research and those with bodies engaged in work feel summoned to work toward an undefined Unity that lies ahead, an immanent god of sorts. So Teilhard found many idealistic people of his time turning to Marxism, for Marxists told of such a god. Teilhard believed the Church could give this god its true name by telling of the cosmic Christ that he found in the writings of St. Paul. This would render the immanent god loving and personal, what the faceless god of Marx never was.

Teilhard was aware of the unsuccessful experiment known as the priest-worker movement in France (priests became factory workers and in the process many left the priesthood). He saw them finding a sacred value in their work of which the Church had nothing to say. Marx articulated this value for many (including some worker-priests). Teilhard found St. Paul articulating this in a more complete and personal way. Marx had idolized a faceless "humanity." To know anyone as a person, the individual must *reveal* one's self. This is what our God has done, revealed himself in the words of Christ—especially the words claiming events as his body and blood. The priest is to show the revelation to scientists and workers of the earth. But Teilhard also had a message for Christian believers: he would urge them to be open to the immanent god they were finding in their work. He asks, "If a man closes his soul against the summons of the immanent Godhead, from what substance will he draw nourishment to keep alive the processes by which he claims to sustain his prayer?"[25]

Both research and work were seen as "conquests," so Teilhard told of "a spirit of conquest," a "passionate desire to conquer the world," "the increasing domination of the world by thought," "the lofty passion of struggle, to know, dominate, or organize."[26] This means we first come upon things that appear incoherent, but this "incoherence is a prelude to unification."[27] "Everything is initially absurd, incoherent (chances); but all can become adorable."[28] Teilhard felt called to work among the realities "esteemed to be the most dangerous, the most unspiritual, the most pagan";[29] he felt drawn to where his faith was most threatened. Without the threat of incoherence there would be no conquests that would enable adoration. Adoration involved all the fibers of "the unifying universe"; and the universe is unify*ing* only as the conquest takes place. Science is a process, not a set of conclusions.

Teilhard would often tell of being refreshed when back in touch with the earth: "I am...in close contact with old mother Earth: and you know that, for me, there is no better way for rejuvenation, and even 'adoration.'"[30] While writing this he was in Africa integrating rock formations into a global picture. But integration is a process, rather than a result achieved. He was not satisfied in simply gazing at nature; this is not research. For Teilhard one can find no rest in nature until one reaches "the ultimate term hidden in it....Perhaps this peculiarity of my sensitivity derives from the fact that things in the cosmos and in life have always presented themselves to me as objects to be pursued and studied,—never just as material for contemplation."[31] We can intuit the soul of another only by an ongoing observation of the other's behavior. So by observing the universe (research) we can intuit its divine Soul. (It is still impersonal; it personalizes itself only by speaking to us—this Teilhard found in the New Testament.) Teilhard did not favor contemplation as a state of rest, for he knew his mind as essentially process. He tells often of difficulty in making the meditations of *The Spiritual Exercises* of St. Ignatius where one tries to rest the mind in a loving contemplation of Jesus.[32] For Teilhard believed God is found in the world's process, its becoming; so in his "Mass" it is *not* the world that is consecrated; it is the world's two processes (growth and diminishment). The world itself serves as the altar.

For Teilhard God operates most intensely in human research, for in research a new level of consciousness emerges. In the philosophic idealism of Teilhard, the world (in us) attains a higher form of being in the new and more inclusive understanding that comes from research. This new world in the mind is "essentially, 'ontologically,' Christifiable"; it is this world that can attain salvation when one makes an act of faith. So Teilhard concludes: "The place for us priests, then, is precisely there, at the point from which all truth and all new power emerges [research]: that so Christ may inform every growth, through man, of the universe in movement."[33]

Research is a process, and, therefore, it takes time; unifying one's understanding is also a process. The apostle Thomas went through a process before he could say, "My Lord and my God." Teilhard feared that theology was frozen in formulas that were simply to be believed (no process) and contemplated. Teilhard had a close Jesuit friend whom he believed held his Catholic faith this way, as a *cassette close*, and quietly went about his academic research, for theology had ceased to engage him. Likewise, those who are *not engaged* in geology would not know adoration by looking at African rocks, for their minds have not been trained or developed along lines that enable them to "conquer" what they see and bring it into a wider understanding. In feeling drawn to assist in a vast unifying process one begins to sense a great Unifying Presence that will appear in the future; then one becomes aware of adoration as a dimension of the research itself. So Teilhard tells of looking for Christ by "communicating with the *Becoming* of things"; "To be in communion with Becoming has become the formula of my whole life."[34] Year after year he concludes his retreat notes with the determination "to communicate with the Becoming,"[35] and spoke of a "communion with time" as the supreme form of adoration.[36] It was not the *being* of a wider unity; it was the *process* of unification (becoming) that enabled adoration. This was evident in his "Mass on the World" as he invoked the divine fire on what would spring up, grow, flower, and ripen, and on what would wither and corrode—all are processes. He would speak of being "in communion with the Becoming under the two species: life-death." The emphasis on process seemed to become clearer as time went on. In 1951, when he thought of rewriting his "Mass," he wrote, "The difference between 'The Mass on the World' in 1923 and now is that I have now put a name on the isolated Cosmic element that is consecratable: Convergence."[37] Convergence is a process. The converging world is in the mind of one doing research (or of one working with matter); the elements in an active mind continually seem to rearrange themselves until they come together to form a new synthesis. So the data in the mind of the scientist seem to be reaching beyond themselves for the hypothesis that will make them one. And each of us finds our mind struggling to "make sense" of our life. And in the process the mind senses a unifying Power greater than its own. In forming wider unities it discovers a mysterious divinity. And Christians too must discover this divinity. For only by an ongoing discovery can their image of Christ be enlarged. "We cannot continue to love Christ without discovering him more and more."[38]

Teilhard acknowledged the prayer of those who simply believed and he himself prayed often in this way. Such prayer is to "pure God" or "pure Omega," but it does not include the "dark adoration" that comes from experience. He prayed to "pure Omega" in doing the customary Catholic devotions: "meditation, breviary, examen and rosary."[39] But note, in his listing of devotions, he does not mention the Mass. For the Mass includes "seeing," and the adoration that is the unity of seeing and believing. In the "Mass," our world (the world we see and touch) is presented in the offertory ("one by one, Lord, I see and I love all those"). Then with faith we *believe* our world is assumed by God ("This is my Body….my Blood"). In the post-communion, seeing and believing act together and we affirm, "My Lord and my God."

Notes

1. HM, 18.
2. HM, 23.
3. HM, 207.
4. HM, 3; A, 281.
5. P, 180.
6. W, 15; D, 46; P, 31.
7. HM, 68.
8. HM, 72–73.
9. HM, 68.

10. HM, 74.
11. HM, 71.
12. C, 118.
13. F, 13; S, 81.
14. HM, 46–47.
15. W, 27; C, 99.
16. S, 214.
17. C, 64.
18. LMF, 196, 149.
19. LJM, 55, 53.
20. LMF, 65.
21. LJM, 14; UL, Carlihan, June 19, 1953.
22. Li, 25.
23. See Cuenot, 133; LJM, 143.
24. LMF, 144; LT, 119.
25. W, 121.
26. Barbour, 111; LT, 274; S, 81; UL, Fontoynont, March 15, 1916.
27. LT, 73.
28. J, April 11, 1952.
29. W, 220.
30. LS, 285.
31. MM, 213–14.
32. Nr, 210, 234.
33. S, 202.
34. LT, 283.
35. Nr, 124.
36. LMF, 153.
37. J, July 17, 1951; see also February 3, 1951.
38. F, 34.
39. Nr, 128.

7.

THE "MASS" AND THE APOSTOLATE

"I have no ability to proclaim anything except the innumer-
able prolongations of your incarnate being."

All his life Teilhard was an apostle, and he ends both "The
Priest" and "The Mass on the World" with an apostolic dedication. In the "Mass" he told of the limits of his mission: "I can
preach only the mystery of your flesh." And this he preached in
season and out. Preaching the flesh of Christ made him a different sort of missionary. The difference could be seen in a note
written in his journal in 1952 on the feast of St. Isaac Jogues and
companions (Jesuit apostles to the Hurons and Iroquois who
were martyred in the 1640s). He reflected that the ideal of "conversion" that had motivated Jogues and others was not his ideal:
"The only thing that counts for me is not to propagate God, but
to discover Him; from this, conversion follows somewhat auto-
matically."[1] When he first observed how the European missionaries worked to convert the Chinese people, he complained,
"The missionaries here are pushing an artificial religion without
a natural trunk."[2] The natural trunk referred to the natural religion the people already had; Christianity should be presented as
the completion and fulfillment of their own world. When his
friends struggled with their faith, he told them they must first
discover the god of their life. He wrote to Lucile Swan, a sculp-
tor: "Your art is, I think, the sacred thread which, if followed,
will lead you to the light which will be *yours*."[3] He would direct
his friends' attention to what their "real me" had been finding
in the world; they must look to the things that had engaged
them (science, art, politics, etc.) and ask where the engagement
was going.

Teilhard the apostle stated it explicitly when he said one should begin conversions by leading people to a *"fuller consciousness of the Universe."*[4] Then show them how their own work in the universe opens their vision to some "crowning glory for the Universe." Only then would he introduce the Christian revelation to people already sensitized "by the religious expectation of some *soul of the World.*"[5] Then he would present the basic content of the revelation by quoting from the Mass, *"Hoc est corpus meum* [This is my Body]." Here, when the body has been located, the words of Christian revelation tell of the Soul laying claim to what has been found; then one's own world, "my universe," is adopted into the final Christ. There is a process people must go through to come to conversion, and the process begins by directing their attention to their world, the world that fascinates them—it was by such a fascination that the World Soul first "summoned" them to come out of themselves. Teilhard believed that the attracting world could find its consummation only in Christ. If their world and its concerns were not involved, they would be unable to worship God *"ex toto corde suo* [with all their hearts]," for they would not have found *their* God. In other terms, he would show them the world they loved was only "flesh" (matter that reveals God, but not to be loved in itself); then he would show them the Soul reflected in matter is Christ. First, he would lead them *to see* and then *to believe.* Thus, his writings that teach us to see are at the heart of his apostolate.

Teilhard kept hoping the official Church would speak of Christ as Soul of the World, such as he found in St. Paul. Should the Church present such a teaching, he believed, many would find in the Church what they were groping toward in their work. Many had come upon a *deo ignoto,* an unknown god, an immanent god about whom they could hardly speak.[6] To such people he would preach as St. Paul preached to the Athenians.

In Athens St. Paul told of seeing an altar dedicated "To an unknown God," and proceeding from there he told the people of Athens, "What therefore you worship as unknown [dark adoration?], this I proclaim to you." He went on to quote an Athenian poet: "In him we live and move and have our being." He quoted *their* inscription and *their* poet, for conversion had to begin with them. He connected the more or less *pantheistic* god (pantheistic: "In him we live and move and have our being") they had found on their own with Jesus. This was an immanent God who desired "that people should feel after him and find him" (Acts 17:23–28; a passage quoted in "Mass on the World"[7]). Teilhard was convinced we (believers and unbelievers) have a sense for god, and he wanted the Church to articulate for people today the god "whom we try to apprehend by the groping of our lives" as St. Paul did for the Athenians.

Today there is a disconnect between religion and spirituality. Religion can be seen as a teaching based upon claims of a revelation; on hearing the words proclaimed, the listener is asked to accept the claim, as the Chinese were asked to accept the words of the missionary. Spirituality involves a careful attention to the many spirits within; it has many forms and these often lead one to a nonjudgmental stance with regards to all revelations. Having a spirituality and no religion (no commitment) some people drift from teacher to guru to prophet, seeking anyone who speaks of a bright, new age that is coming. There are many New Age gurus today who articulate a vision of a bright future and an immanent god, and their disciples resonate to the message. Many New Age leaders consider Teilhard highly influential in their thinking.****
Teilhard believed that the Church should be articulating the vision. For the Church has what the New Age disciples do not

---

**** See Marilyn Ferguson's *The Aquarian Conspiracy: Personal and Social Transformations in the 1980s* (Los Angeles: J. P. Tarcher, 1980 and 1987). She tells of interviewing 185 leaders of the New Age movement. When asked who was most influential in their thinking, the name most frequently mentioned was Teilhard de Chardin. He has much in common with them in their concern for the earth, their cosmic ways of thinking, their look to a bright future, and so forth. But there are two ways Teilhard differs from the New Age gurus and their disciples. First, suffering and death were integral to the thought of Teilhard, while these are rarely considered by those of the New Age. Second, Teilhard gave his life a central commitment, while those in the New Age generally remain open to all and committed to none.

have and perhaps do not want: commitment. Many of those of the New Age are "free spirits" who drift about unwilling to commit themselves, for the spirits within them are many and transient. Such people generally acknowledge Jesus as a great teacher and even a friend (much as Teilhard had done), but beyond this they look for someone to identify *the immanent god they have found* in the groping of their lives. Teilhard believed we are all groping for the Soul that will unite us. The desire for unity is fundamental to our human identity ("Man is not drawn towards the One...by his reason alone, but by the full force of his whole being"[8]), so people everywhere are calling out, "Lord, make us one." That is, they are yearning for a Soul that will unite their own divided spirits and in so doing unite the human family. This yearning is the "natural trunk" that must be identified and addressed by the gospel. When this is done Teilhard believed that the Christian message would follow naturally and Christ as Soul of the World would satisfy what those of the New Age are seeking. That is, they could find this Soul through sharing in the Christian priesthood he presented in his "Mass."

All Christians know the troubled world of today, for it has settled into the depths of their souls. To deal with it they must know their priestly identity. This means that over the divided and hope-filled world gathered onto their patens (souls) they can say the words given us by God, "This is my Body." And in this act of faith many of the spirits within them attain their unified Soul. And with this one *sees* Christ everywhere.

But in saying, "*many* of the spirits...attain their unified Soul," what of the rest?

There is a second part to the communion, and to stop with the first part, one's "*communion would be incomplete—would, quite simply, not be Christian.*" One must accept the processes "*of enfeeblement, of aging, of death, which unceasingly consume the universe.*" These too have become spirit in us. Over the dread elements of failure and death one is called to repeat the other priestly words given us by God, "This is my Blood." Then, as we proceed through the day, even our defeats will be moments of communion. Each day we will be asked to take a sip from the cup, knowing each day leads to our death. In this second part of our journey into God, all seeing is left behind. At this point Teilhard would agree with St. John of the Cross and the more traditional Christian asceticism. Now for all of us, "Blessed are those who believe without seeing." The day also will come when we are asked to take more than a sip from the chalice; one day we will be told to drink it to the bitter end, that is, to the point of annihilation where all sense of self ("real me" and so forth) is lost and *nothing is seen*: it is *"the supreme mystery of faith."*

In 1947 Teilhard suffered a cardiac infarction and for ten days hesitated between life and death. In his next annual retreat (1948) he wrote of a "communion through death," and in simpler terms called it, "the Death Communion."[10] This is our annihilation, when our communion is completed. In the Mass, Christ is both the priest that makes the offering and the victim that must be sacrificed. And each Christian is the same.

One has known the world as Christ's body, but the moment comes when Jesus extends the cup to us, "Drink ye all of this." It is an awesome moment, but the one *"filled with an impassioned love for Jesus hidden in the forces which bring death to the earth, him the earth will clasp in the immensity of her arms as her strength fails, and with her he will awaken in the bosom of God."*

The Death Communion is the supreme mystery of faith. For in drinking from the cup there is no tangible compensation. Teilhard could first understand his ordination during the carnage of World War I: there he spoke of death as the *logical crowning of the priesthood*. And for all of us our death is that. For essentially every Christian is a priest and our life constitutes the great Mass each is called to offer on the altar of the world. But in the Mass Christ, the priest, is also the victim that must be sacrificed! Each believer is the same: by our death we are sacrificed in Christ and as Christ. As Christ? It is the Death Communion; now we are One.

> Happy are those among us who, in these decisive days of the creation and redemption, have been chosen for this supreme act, the logical crowning of their priest-

hood: to be in communion, even unto death, with the Christ who is being born and suffering in the human race.[11]

Teach me to treat my death as an act of communion.[12]

There is something highly exalting in Christian death: to find Him…what a thrill![13]

Notes

1. UJ, September 26, 1952; see also UJ, July 13, 1951.
2. UL, Gaudefroy, August 15, 1923.
3. LS, 1.
4. HM, 214; italics in text.
5. HM, 215.
6. F, 25.
7. HM, 124; D, 46–47.
8. C, 57.
9. HM, 130.
10. Nr, 284.
11. W, 224.
12. D, 90.
13. Nr, 223.

Appendix I:
"THE MASS ON THE WORLD"
by Teilhard de Chardin

The Offering

Since once again, Lord—though this time not in the forests of the Aisne but in the steppes of Asia—I have neither bread, nor wine, nor altar, I will raise myself beyond these symbols, up to the pure majesty of the real itself; I, your priest, will make the whole earth my altar and on it will offer you all the labours and sufferings of the world.

Over there, on the horizon, the sun has just touched with light the outermost fringe of the eastern sky. Once again, beneath this moving sheet of fire, the living surface of the earth wakes and trembles, and once again begins its fearful travail. I will place on my paten, O God, the harvest to be won by this renewal of labour. Into my chalice I shall pour all the sap which is to be pressed out this day from the earth's fruits.

My paten and my chalice are the depths of a soul laid widely open to all the forces which in a moment will rise up from every corner of the earth and converge upon the Spirit. Grant me the remembrance and the mystic presence of all those whom the light is now awakening to the new day.

One by one, Lord, I see and I love all those whom you have given me to sustain and charm my life. One by one also I number all those who make up that other beloved family which has gradually surrounded me, its unity fashioned out of the most disparate elements, with affinities of the heart, of scientific research and of thought. And again one by one—more vaguely it is true, yet all-inclusively—I call before me the whole vast anonymous army of living humanity; those who surround me and support me though

145

I do not know them; those who come, and those who go; above all, those who in office, laboratory and factory, through their vision of truth or despite their error, truly believe in the progress of earthly reality and who today will take up again their impassioned pursuit of the light.

This restless multitude, confused or orderly, the immensity of which terrifies us; this ocean of humanity whose slow, monotonous wave-flows trouble the hearts even of those whose faith is most firm: it is to this deep that I thus desire all the fibres of my being should respond. All the things in the world to which this day will bring increase; all those that will diminish; all those too that will die: all of them, Lord, I try to gather into my arms, so as to hold them out to you in offering. This is the material of my sacrifice; the only material you desire.

Once upon a time men took into your temple the first fruits of their harvests, the flower of their flocks. But the offering you really want, the offering you mysteriously need every day to appease your hunger, to slake your thirst is nothing less than the growth of the world borne ever onwards in the stream of universal becoming.

Receive, O Lord, this all-embracing host which your whole creation, moved by your magnetism, offers you at this dawn of a new day.

This bread, our toil, is of itself, I know, but an immense fragmentation; this wine, our pain, is no more, I know, than a draught that dissolves. Yet in the very depths of this formless mass you have implanted—and this I am sure of, for I sense it—a desire, irresistible, hallowing, which makes us cry out, believer and unbeliever alike: "Lord, make us *one*."

Because, my God, though I lack the soul-zeal and the sublime integrity of your saints, I yet have received from you an overwhelming sympathy for all that stirs within the dark mass of matter; because I know myself to be irremediably less a child of heaven than a son of earth; therefore I will this morning climb up in spirit to the high places, bearing with me the hopes and the miseries of my mother; and there—empowered by that priesthood which you alone (as I firmly believe) have bestowed on me—upon all that in the world of human flesh is now about to be born or to die beneath the rising sun I will call down the Fire.

Fire Over the Earth

Fire, the source of being: we cling so tenaciously to the illusion that fire comes forth from the depths of the earth and that its flames grow progressively brighter as it pours along the radiant furrows of life's tillage. Lord, in your mercy you gave me to see that this idea is false, and that I must overthrow it if I were ever to have sight of you.

In the beginning was *Power*, intelligent, loving, energizing. In the beginning was the *Word*, supremely capable of mastering and moulding whatever might come into being in the world of matter. In the beginning there were not coldness and darkness: there was the *Fire*. This is the truth.

So, far from light emerging gradually out of the womb of our darkness, it is the Light, existing before all else was made which, patiently, surely, eliminates our darkness. As for us creatures, of ourselves we are but emptiness and obscurity. But you, my God, are the inmost depths, the stability of that eternal *milieu*, without duration or space, in which our cosmos emerges gradually into being and grows gradually to its final completeness, as it loses those boundaries which to our eyes seem so immense. Everything is being; everywhere there is being and nothing but being, save in the fragmentation of creatures and the clash of their atoms.

Blazing Spirit, Fire, personal, supersubstantial, the consummation of a union so immeasurably more lovely and more desirable than that destructive fusion of which all the pantheists dream: be pleased yet once again to come down and breathe a soul into the newly formed, fragile film of matter with which this day the world is to be freshly clothed.

I know we cannot forestall, still less dictate to you, even the smallest of your actions; from you alone comes all initiative—and this applies in the first place to my prayer.

Radiant Word, blazing Power, you who mould the multiple so as to breathe your life into it; I pray you, lay on us those your hands—powerful, considerate, omnipresent, those hands which do not (like our human hands) touch now here, now there, but which plunge into the depths and the totality, present and past, of things so as to reach us simultaneously through all that is most immense and most inward within us and around us.

May the might of those invincible hands direct and transfigure for the great world you have in mind that earthly travail which I have gathered into my heart and now offer you in its entirety. Remould it, rectify it, recast it down to the depths from whence it springs. You know how your creatures can come into being only, like shoot from stem, as part of an endlessly renewed process of evolution.

Do you now therefore, speaking through my lips, pronounce over this earthly travail your twofold efficacious word: the word without which all that our wisdom and our experience have built up must totter and crumble—the word through which all our most far-reaching speculations and our encounter with the universe are come together into a unity. Over every living thing which is to spring up, to grow, to flower, to ripen during this day say again the words: This is my Body. And over every death-force which waits in readiness to corrode, to wither, to cut down, speak again your commanding words which express the supreme mystery of faith: This is my Blood.

Fire In the Earth

It is done.

Once again the Fire has penetrated the earth.

Not with sudden crash of thunderbolt, riving the mountaintops: does the Master break down doors to enter his own home? Without earthquake, or thunderclap: the flame has lit up the whole world from within. All things individually and collectively are penetrated and flooded by it, from the inmost core of the tiniest atom to the mighty sweep of the most universal laws of being:

so naturally has it flooded every element, every energy, every connecting-link in the unity of our cosmos; that one might suppose the cosmos to have burst spontaneously into flame.

In the new humanity which is begotten today the Word prolongs the unending act of his own birth; and by virtue of his immersion in the world's womb the great waters of the kingdom of matter have, without even a ripple, been endued with life. No visible tremor marks this inexpressible transformation; and yet, mysteriously and in every truth, at the touch of the supersubstantial Word the immense host which is the universe is made flesh. Through your own incarnation, my God, all matter is henceforth incarnate.

Through our thoughts and our human experiences, we long ago became aware of the strange properties which make the universe so like our flesh: like the flesh it attracts us by the charm which lies in the mystery of its curves and folds and in the depths of its eyes; like the flesh it disintegrates and eludes us when submitted to our analyses or to our fallings away and in the process of its own perdurance; as with the flesh, it can only be embraced in the endless reaching out to attain what lies beyond the confines of what has been given to us.

All of us, Lord, from the moment we are born feel within us this disturbing mixture of remoteness and nearness; and in our heritage of sorrow and hope, passed down to us through the ages, there is no earning more desolate than that which makes us weep with vexation and desire as we stand in the midst of the Presence which hovers about us nameless and impalpable and is indwelling in all things. *Si forte attrectent eum.*

Now, Lord, through the consecration of the world the luminosity and fragrance which suffuse the universe take on for me the lineaments of a body and a face—in you. What my mind glimpsed through its hesitant explorations, what my heart craved with so little expectation of fulfilment, you now magnificently unfold for me: the fact that your creatures are not merely so linked together in solidarity that none can exist unless all the rest surround it, but that all are so dependent on a single central reality that a true life, borne in common by them all, gives them ultimately their consistence and their unity.

Shatter, my God, through the daring of your revelation the childishly timid outlook that can conceive of nothing greater or more vital in the world than the pitiable perfection of our human organism. On the road to a bolder comprehension of the universe the children of this world day by day outdistance the masters of Israel; but do you, Lord Jesus, "in whom all things subsist," show yourself to those who love you as the higher Soul and the physical centre of your creation? Are you not well aware that for us this is a question of life or death? As for me, if I could not believe that your real presence animates and makes tractable and enkindles even the very least of the energies which invade me or brush past me, would I not die of cold?

I thank you, my God, for having in a thousand different ways led my eyes to discover the immense simplicity of things. Little by little, through the irresistible development of those yearnings you implanted in me as a child, through the influence of gifted friends who entered my life at certain moments to bring light and strength to my mind, and through the awakenings of spirit I owe to the successive initiations, gentle and terrible, which you caused me to undergo: through all these I have been brought to the point where I can no longer see anything, nor any longer breathe, outside that *milieu* in which all is made one.

At this moment when your life has just poured with superabundant vigour into the sacrament of the world, I shall savour with heightened consciousness the intense yet tranquil rapture of a vision whose coherence and harmonies I can never exhaust.

What I experience as I stand in face of—and in the very depths of—this world which your flesh has assimilated, this world which has become your flesh, my God, is not the absorption of the monist who yearns to be dissolved into the unity of things, nor the emotion felt by the pagan as he lies prostrate before a tangible divinity, nor yet the passive self-abandonment of the quietist tossed hither and thither at the mercy of mystical impulsions. From each of these modes of thought I take something of their motive force while avoiding their pitfalls: the approach determined for me by your omnipresence is a wonderful synthesis wherein three of the most formidable passions that can unlock the human heart rectify each other as they mingle: like the monist I plunge into the all-inclusive One; but the One is so perfect that as it receives me and I lose myself in it I can find in it the ultimate perfection of my own individuality; like the pagan I worship a God who can be touched; and I do indeed touch him—this God—over the whole surface and in the depths of that world of matter which confines me: but to take hold of him as I would wish (simply in order not to stop touching him), I must go always on and on through and beyond each undertaking, unable to rest in anything, borne onwards at each moment by creatures and at each moment going beyond them, in a continuing welcoming of them and a continuing detachment from them; like the quietist I allow myself with delight to be cradled in the divine fantasy: but at the same time I know that the divine will, will only be revealed to me at each moment if I exert myself to the utmost: I shall only touch God in the world of matter, when, like Jacob, I have been vanquished by him.

Thus, because the ultimate objective, the totality to which my nature is attuned has been made manifest to me, the powers of my being begin spontaneously to vibrate in accord with a single note of incredible richness wherein I can distinguish the most discordant tendencies effortlessly resolved: the excitement of action and the delight of passivity: the joy of possessing and the thrill of reaching out beyond what one possesses; the pride in growing and the happiness of being lost in what is greater than oneself.

Rich with the sap of the world, I rise up towards the Spirit whose vesture is the magnificence of the material universe but who smiles at me from far beyond all victories; and, lost in the mystery of the flesh of God, I cannot tell which is the more radiant bliss: to have found the Word and so be able to achieve the mastery of matter, or to have mastered matter and so be able to attain and submit to the light of God.

Grant, Lord, that your descent into the universal Species may not be for me just something loved and cherished, like the fruit of some philosophical speculation, but may become for me truly a real Presence. Whether we like it or not by power and by right you are incarnate in the world and we are all of us dependent upon you. But in fact you are far, and how far, from being equally close to us all. We are all of us together carried in the one world-womb; yet each of us is our own little microcosm in which the Incarnation is wrought independently with degrees of intensity, and shades that are incommunicable. And that is why, in our prayer at the altar, we ask that the consecration may be brought about *for us: Ut nobis Corpus et Sanguis fiat...*If I firmly believe that everything around me is the body and blood of the Word, then for me (and in one sense for me alone) is brought about that marvellous "diaphany" which causes the luminous warmth of a single life to be objectively discernible in and to shine forth from the depths of every event, every element: whereas if, unhappily, my faith should flag, at once the light is quenched and everything becomes darkened, everything disintegrates.

You have come down, Lord, into this day which is now beginning. But alas, how infinitely different in degree is your presence for one and another of us in the events which are now preparing and which all of us together will experience! In the very same circumstances which are soon to surround me and my fellowmen you may be present in small measure, in great measure, more and more or not at all.

Therefore, Lord, that no poison may harm me this day, no death destroy me, no wine befuddle me, that in every creature I may discover and sense you, I beg you: give me faith.

Communion

If the Fire has come down into the heart of the world it is, in the last resort, to lay hold on me and to absorb me. Henceforth I cannot be content simply to contemplate it or, by my steadfast faith, to intensify its ardency more and more in the world around me. What I must do, when I have taken part with all my energies in the consecration which causes its flames to leap forth, is to consent to the communion which will enable it to find in me the food it has come in the last resort to seek.

So, my God, I prostrate myself before your presence in the universe which has now become living flame: beneath the lineaments of all that I shall encounter this day, all that happens to me, all that I achieve, it is you I desire, you I await.

It is a terrifying thing to have been born: I mean, to find oneself, without having willed it, swept irrevocably along on a torrent of fearful energy which seems as though it wished to destroy everything it carries with it.

What I want, my God, is that by a reversal of forces which you alone can bring about, my terror in face of the nameless changes destined to renew my being may be turned into an overflowing joy at being transformed into you.

First of all I shall stretch out my hand unhesitatingly towards the fiery bread which you set before me. This bread, in which you have planted the seed of all that is to develop in the future, I recognize as containing the source and the secret of that destiny you have chosen for me. To take it is, I know, to surrender myself to forces which will tear me away painfully from myself in order to drive me into danger, into laborious undertakings, into a constant renewal of ideas, into an austere detachment where my affections are concerned. To eat it is to acquire a taste and an affinity for that which in everything is above everything— a taste and an affinity which will henceforward make impossible for me all the joys by which my life has been warmed. Lord Jesus, I am willing to be possessed by you, to be bound to your body and led by its inexpressible power towards those solitary heights which by myself I should never dare to climb. Instinctively, like all mankind, I would rather set up my tent here below on some hill-top of my own choosing. I am afraid, too, like all my fellowmen, of the future too heavy with mystery and too wholly new, toward which time is driving me. Then like these men I wonder anxiously where life is leading me...May this communion of bread with the Christ clothed in the powers which dilate the world free me from my timidities and my heedlessness! In the whirlpool of conflicts and energies out of which must develop my power to apprehend and experience your holy presence, I throw myself, my God, on your word. The man who is filled with an impassioned love of Jesus hidden in the forces which bring increase to the earth, him the earth will lift up, like a mother, in the immensity of her arms, and will enable him to contemplate the face of God.

If your kingdom, my God, were of this world, I could possess you simply by surrendering myself to the forces which cause us, through suffering and dying, to grow visibly in stature—us or that which is dearer to us than ourselves. But because the term towards which the earth is moving lies not merely beyond each individual thing but beyond the totality of things; because the world travails, not to bring forth from within itself some supreme reality, but to find its consummation through a union with a pre-existent Being; it follows that man can never reach the blazing centre of the universe simply by living more and more for himself nor even by spending his life in the service of some earthly cause however great. The world can never be definitively united with you, Lord, save by a sort of reversal, a turning about, an *excentration*, which must involve the temporary collapse not merely of all individual achievements but even of everything that looks like an advancement for humanity. If my being is ever to be decisively attached to yours, there must first die in me not merely the monad ego but also the world: in other words I must first pass through an agonizing phase of diminution for which no tangible compensation will be given me. That is why, pouring into my chalice the bitterness of all separations, of all limitations, and of all sterile fallings away, you then hold it out to me, "Drink ye all of this."

How could I refuse this chalice, Lord, now that through the bread you have given me there has crept into the marrow of my being an inextinguishable longing to be united with you beyond life; through death? The consecration of the world would have remained incomplete, a moment ago, had you not with special love vitalized for those who believe, not only the life-bringing forces, but also those which bring death. My communion would be incomplete—would, quite simply, not be christian—if, together with the gains which this new day brings me, I did not also accept, in my own name and in the name of the world, as the most immediate sharing in your own being, those processes, hidden or manifest, of enfeeblement, of ageing, of death, which unceasingly consume the universe, to its salvation or its condemnation. My God, I deliver myself up with utter abandon to those fearful forces of dissolution which, I blindly believe, will this day cause my narrow ego to be replaced by your divine presence. This man who is filled with an impassioned love for Jesus hidden in the forces which bring death to the earth, him the earth will clasp in the immensity of her arms as her strength fails, and with her he will awaken in the bosom of God.

Prayer

Lord Jesus, now that beneath those world-forces you have become truly and physically everything for me, everything about me, everything within me, I shall gather into a single prayer both my delight in what I have and my thirst for what I lack; and following the lead of your great servant I shall repeat those enflamed words in which, I firmly believe, the christianity of tomorrow will find its increasingly clear portrayal:

"Lord, lock me up in the deepest depths of your heart; and then, holding me there, burn me, purify me, set me on fire, sublimate me, till I become utterly what you would have me be, through the utter annihilation of my ego."

Tu autem, Domine mi, include me in imis visceribus Cordis tui. Atque ibi me detine, excoque, expurga, accende, ignifac, sublima, ad purissimum Cordis tui gustum atque placitum, ad puram annihilationem meam.

"Lord." Yes, at last, through the twofold mystery of this universal consecration and communion I have found one to whom I can wholeheartedly give this name. As long as I could see—or dared to see—in you, Lord Jesus, only the man who lived two thousand years ago, the sublime moral teacher, the Friend, the Brother, my love remained timid and constrained. Friends, brothers, wise men: have we not many of these around us, great souls, chosen souls, and much closer to us? And then can man ever give himself utterly to a nature which is purely human? Always from the very first it was the world, greater than all the elements which make up the world, that I was in love with; and never before was there anyone before whom I could in honesty bow down. And so for a long time, even though I believed, I strayed, not knowing what it was I loved. But now, Master, today, when through the manifestation of those superhuman powers with which your resurrection endowed you you shine forth from within all the forces of the earth and so become visible to me, now I recognize you as my Sovereign, and with delight I surrender myself to you.

How strange, my God, are the processes your Spirit initiates! When, two centuries ago, your Church began to feel the particular power of your heart, it might have seemed that what was captivating men's souls was the fact of their finding in you an element even more determinate, more circumscribed, than your humanity as a whole. But now on the contrary a swift reversal is making us aware that your main purpose in this revealing to us of your heart was to enable our love to escape from the constrictions of the too narrow, too precise, too limited image of you which we had fashioned for ourselves. What I discern in your breast is simply a furnace of fire; and the more I fix my gaze on its ardency the more it seems to me that all around it the contours of your body melt away and become enlarged beyond all measure, till the only features I can distinguish in you are those of the face of a world which has burst into flame.

Glorious Lord Christ: the divine influence secretly diffused and active in the depths of matter, and the dazzling centre where all the innumerable fibres of the multiple meet; power as implacable as the world and as warm as life; you whose forehead is of the whiteness of snow, whose eyes are on fire, and whose feet are brighter than molten gold; you whose hands imprison the stars; you who are the first and the last, the living and the dead and the risen again; you who gather into your exuberant unity every beauty, every affinity, every energy, every mode of existence; it is you to whom my being cried out with a desire as vast as the universe, "In truth you are my Lord and my God."

"Lord, lock me up within you": yes indeed I believe—and this belief is so strong that it has become one of the supports of my inner life—that an "exterior darkness" which was wholly outside you would be pure nothingness. Nothing, Lord Jesus, can subsist outside of your flesh; so that even those who have been cast out from your love are still, unhappily for them, the beneficiaries of your presence upholding them in existence. All of us, inescapably, exist in you, the universal *milieu* in which and through which all things live and have their being. But precisely because we are not self-contained ready-made entities which can be conceived equally well as being near to you or remote from you; precisely because in us the self-subsistent individual who is united to you grows only in so far as the union itself grows, that union whereby we are given more and more completely to you: I beg you, Lord, in the name of all that is most vital in my being, to hearken to the desire of this thing that I dare to call *my* soul even though I realize more and more every day how much greater it is than myself, and, to slake my thirst for life, draw me—through the successive zones of your deepest substance—into the secret recesses of your inmost heart.

The deeper the level at which one encounters you, Master, the more one realizes the universality of your influence. This is the criterion by which I can judge at each moment how far I have progressed within you. When all the things around me, while preserving their own individual contours, their own special savours, nevertheless appear to me as animated by a single secret spirit and therefore as diffused and intermingled within a single element, infinitely close, infinitely remote; and when, locked within the jealous intimacy of a divine sanctuary, I yet feel myself to be wandering at large in the empyrean of all created beings: then I shall know that I am approaching that central point where the heart of the world is caught in the descending radiance of the heart of God.

And then, Lord, at that point where all things are set ablaze, do you act upon me through the united flames of all those internal and external influences which, were I less close to you, would be neutral or ambivalent or hostile, but which when animated by an Energy *quae possit sibi omnia subjicere* become, in the physical depths of your heart, the angels of your triumphant activity. Through a marvellous combination of your divine magnetism with the charm and the inadequacy of creatures, with their sweetness and their malice, their disappointing weakness and their terrifying power, do you fill my heart alternately with exaltation and with distaste; teach it the true meaning of purity: not a debilitating separation from all created reality but an impulse carrying one through all forms of created beauty; show it the true nature of charity: not a sterile fear of doing wrong but a vigorous determination that all of us together shall break open the doors of life; and give it finally—give it above all—through an ever-increasing awareness on your omnipresence, a blessed desire to go on advancing, discovering, fashioning and experiencing the world so as to penetrate ever further and further into yourself.

For me, my God, all joy and all achievement, the very purpose of my being and all my love of life, all depend on this one basic vision of the union between yourself and the universe. Let others, fulfilling a function more august than mine, proclaim your splendours as pure Spirit; as for me, dominated as I am by a vocation which springs from the inmost fibres of my being, I have no desire, I have no ability, to proclaim anything except the innumerable prolongations of your incarnate Being in the world of matter; I can preach only the mystery of your flesh, you the Soul shining forth through all that surrounds us.

It is to your body in this its fullest extension—that is, to the world become through your power and my faith the glorious living crucible in which everything melts away in order to be born anew; it is to this that I dedicate myself with all the resources which your creative magnetism has brought forth in me: with the all too feeble resources of my scientific knowledge, with my religious vows, with my priesthood, and (most dear to me) with my deepest human convictions. It is in this dedication, Lord Jesus, I desire to live, in this I desire to die.

Ordos, 1923

Appendix II:
A PRAYER SERVICE BASED ON "THE MASS ON THE WORLD"

The following text can stand on its own as a prayer service or—as Teilhard spoke of the extensions of the Eucharist—it can be used as an extension of the Mass. This can be done without interrupting the Mass by having passages read before the Mass begins, other passages read before the offertory, other passages at the communion, and yet others as the Mass comes to an end. To have the congregation read them at communion would not violate the integrity of the Mass, as at this time the congregation often sings a hymn. That would leave one short passage that could be read before the preface, or else at the end of the offertory.

The text is based on Teilhard's "Mass on the World." The sentences have been shortened and modified to make the text more widely accessible. Teilhard's "Mass" was offered at sunrise and that is the best time to celebrate it. But sometimes it fits better into schedules if it is offered as part of an evening program. An alternative opening text is placed in brackets for use in the evening. During the longer passages a musician could softly play the guitar.

Priest/Leader:

Over there on the horizon, the sun has just touched with light the outermost fringe of the eastern sky.

Once again, beneath this moving sheet of fire, the living surface of the earth wakes and trembles and begins its fearful travail.

Lord, I your priest will make the whole earth my altar and on it I will offer you the labors and sufferings of the coming day.

[The outermost fringe of the western sky has darkened and our human world has settled again into silence. This evening, Lord, I your priest will make the whole earth my altar and on it I will offer you the labors and sufferings of the coming day.]

Congregation:

One by one, Lord, we envision around us all those whom you have given us to sustain and charm our lives.

One by one also we number all those who make up another beloved family that has surrounded us, its unity fashioned out of the most disparate elements with affinities of the heart, of research, and of thought.

And again one by one we call before us the whole vast army of living humanity, those who support us though we do not know them; those who through their vision of truth or despite their error will take up again their impassioned pursuit of the Light.

This restless ocean of humanity terrifies us; its immensity troubles the hearts of those whose faith is most firm.

But it is to the human multitude that we desire all the depths of our being to respond.

All the things that the coming day will bring increase, and all the things that will wither and die, all of them, Lord, we gather into our arms and hold them out to you in offering. This is the material you desire.

Priest/Leader:

Lord, I find I have received from you an overwhelming sympathy for all that stirs in the dark heart of matter.

I know myself irremediably less a child of heaven than I am a child of this earth.

But I let my spirit climb to the high places bearing within it the hopes and the miseries of the earth, my mother. And there at the heights of spirit and empowered by the priesthood that you alone have bestowed upon me, upon all that is about to be born and upon all that is about to die I will call down your fire.

Lord, each day in the Mass you lay claim to our earth and it will become your body. And that means the world all around us has become your flesh.

Through our human experience we have gradually become aware of the properties that make the universe so like our human flesh.

Like the flesh the universe attracts us by a charm that lies hidden in mystery.

Like the flesh it disintegrates and eludes us when submitted to analysis.

And like the flesh it can be embraced only by reaching out endlessly to attain that which lies beyond the world already given.

All of us, Lord, from the moment we are born, feel within us a disturbing mixture of remoteness and nearness.

And in the heritage of sorrow and hope passed down to us through the ages, there is no yearning more desolate than that which makes us weep with vexation and desire as we stand in the presence of a spirit that hovers about us nameless and impalpable.

Lord Jesus, let this spirit take on a name and a face in you. Show yourself to those who love you as the very soul and center of your creation. Are you not aware that for me this is a question of life and death? If I could not believe that your real presence animates every least energy that invades me, would I not die of the cold?

Congregation:

Blazing Spirit, Fire, Personal, Supersubstantial, be pleased once again to come down and breathe a soul of fire into the fragile film of matter with which the world will be freshly clothed.

May the might of your powerful and omnipresent hands remold, rectify, and recast our earthly labor.

Transform our human works into the Great Work you have in mind.

Here, if the service is said together with a Mass, the Mass proper can begin. Suggested readings are Romans 8:19–23 and Matthew 14:22–33; these were favorite readings of Teilhard. Another set of readings would be Acts 17:22–28 and John 20:24–29; these were also favorites of Teilhard and the material for the sermons could be found in the section of the present text in the chapters titled, "The Mass and Adoration" and "The Mass and the Apostolate."

As the gifts are presented at the altar, the priest can say,

Priest/Leader:

I will place upon my paten, O God, the harvest that will be won by today's renewal of labor.

Into my chalice I will pour all the sap that will be pressed painfully from the earth's fruits. My paten and chalice are the depths of a soul laid widely open to all the forces that rise from the earth and converge upon the spirit.

Congregation: *(If said together with a Mass the congregation can say the following words as the priest first holds up the Host and then the chalice. At the same time the priest could say the offertory prayers in silence.)*

Receive, O Lord, this all-embracing Host that your whole creation moved by your magnetism offers you this day.

This wine, our pain, is no more than a drink that dissolves.

But in the depths of these formless masses you have implanted a desire, irresistible and hallowing, which makes us cry out, believer and nonbeliever alike, "Lord, make us one."

(If said together with a Mass, after the washing of the hands a lector could read the following:)

Lector:

Over every living thing that will spring up, grow, flower, and ripen during the course of this day, say again the words, "This is my Body."

Over every death force that waits in readiness to corrode, wither, and cut down, speak again the commanding words that express the supreme mystery of faith, "This is my Blood."

(Then, if together with a Mass, the preface, the sanctus, and the canon. Then the Lord's Prayer, greeting of peace, and the Agnus Dei. As communion approaches the lector can read:)

Lector:

It is a terrifying thing to be born, I mean, to find one's self, without ever having willed it, swept along in a torrent of events that seems to create and then destroy all that has ever lived.

I ask, my God, in the face of the nameless changes that will come to me in the course of the coming day that I may be transformed into you.

(If together with a Mass it would be good to have all receive the Host and then all receive from the chalice.)

Congregation:

We stretch out our hands toward the fiery bread that you have set before us. We know to take it is to surrender ourselves to the forces that dilate the universe.

But those who love you, Jesus, hidden in the forces that bring increase to the earth, the earth will lift up and enable them to contemplate the face of God. *(Reception of the Host)*

If your kingdom, O God, were of this world, we could possess you simply by surrendering ourselves to the forces that cause us to grow visibly in stature.

But you pour into our chalice the bitterness of all separations, of all limitations, and of all sterile fallings away, then you hold it out to us.

"Drink ye all of this. This is the cup of my blood." *(Reception of the chalice—the altar is cleared)*

Priest/Leader:

The consecration of the world would have been incomplete, had you not with special love vitalized not only the life-bringing forces, but also those that bring death.

My communion would have been incomplete, would not have been Christian, if together with the gains the new day brings me, I did not also accept those processes of enfeeblement, aging, and death, which unceasingly consume the universe to its salvation or to its condemnation.

The one who is filled with an impassioned love for Jesus in the forces that bring death to the earth, him the earth will clasp in her arms, and, as her strength fails, with her he will awaken in the bosom of God.

Lord Jesus, as long as I could see—or dared to see in you—only the man who lived two thousand years ago, the sublime moral teacher, the friend, the brother, my love for you remained timid and restrained.

As early as I can remember, it was the world that I loved, and never before was there anyone before whom I could honestly bow down.

And so for a long time—even though I did believe—I strayed, not knowing what it was that I loved.

But today, Master, when through the power of your resurrection you shine forth from all the forces within the earth, you have become visible to me.

And I recognize you as my sovereign.

Within you I discern a furnace of fire.

And the more I fix my gaze on the ardency of your heart, the more it seems to me that all around it the contours of your body become enlarged beyond all measure until the only features I can discern in you is the face of the world that has burst into flame.

Congregation:

Glorious Lord Christ, the divine influence active in the depths of matter and the dazzling center where the fibers meet: power as implacable as the world and power as warm as life.

You whose forehead is of the whiteness of snow, whose eyes are of fire, and whose feet are brighter than molten gold.

You whose hands imprison the stars, you are the first and the last, the living, the dead, and the risen again.

It is you to whom my being cries out with a desire as vast as the universe, "In truth, you are my Lord and my God."

Priest/Leader:

Fill my heart alternately with exaltation and distaste.

Teach my heart the true meaning of purity—not a debilitating separation from all created reality, but an impulse carrying us through all forms of created beauty.

Show me the true nature of charity—not a sterile fear of doing wrong, but a vigorous determination that all of us by working together may open the gates of life.

Finally, and this above all, give me a blessed desire to go on discovering, fashioning, and experiencing the world so as to penetrate further into yourself.

Congregation:

For me, my God, all joy and all achievement, the very purpose of my being and all my love of life, depend on this one basic vision of the union between yourself and the universe.

Let others—fulfilling a function more august than mine—proclaim your splendors as pure spirit.

As for me, dominated as I am by a vocation that springs from the innermost fibers of my being, I have no ability to proclaim anything but the prolongations of your incarnate being.

I can preach only the mystery of your flesh, and you as the Soul shining through everything that surrounds me.

Priest/Leader:

It is to your body in this its fullest extension, that is, to the world become through your power and my faith the glorious living crucible in which everything melts away in order to be born anew; It is to this that I dedicate myself with the feeble resources of my scientific knowledge, with my religious vows, with my priesthood, and—most dear to me—my deepest human convictions.

In this dedication, Lord Jesus, I desire to live; in this dedication I desire to die.

Appendix III:

TO PRAY AS TEILHARD PRAYED

The prayer of Teilhard can be seen as patterned on the Mass, with the format of offertory, consecration, and communion.

In the offertory we recall all the things that concern us. We begin by recalling our hopes and the hopes of those who mean much to us; we should be specific and even detailed about what has been on our minds. Then we recall humanity and its hopes, and the earth and its hungers, as they have become our concerns. All of these we hold out to God. Then we consider our miseries and the miseries of those who mean much to us; the suffering of others all over the globe, and the suffering of the natural world. Again, we consider these in some detail. All of these constitute our world. In the offertory we present our world, the world as we know it, to God. And in doing so we hear all these elements crying out for a common Soul. Is it the elements of things or elements of our selves? It is a cry that arises from our divided depths; it is that which is *in nobis, sine nobis*.

God accepts the offering; this occurs in the consecration. Jesus says over our world in its growing, flowering, and ripening, "This is my Body." Then he says over our world as it corrodes, withers, and is cut down, "This is my Blood."

With that our lives can become a sacrament. For every event is now a communion, as Jesus has claimed all events as either his body or his blood. Jesus has taken our concerns into himself; when this happens, he truly becomes "Our Lord," as he is Lord of the world we know. And with that our world should look different. For we see all around us as the flesh of his body, and the failures we know are his flesh shedding blood.

In ending our prayer and taking up again the concerns of the day, we return to our familiar hopes and miseries. But we know them in a different way; now they are Christ's concerns. As the events of the day unfold, we must recall that each moment has been consecrated and we can say of each, "This is his body," or "This is his blood." And all the events of the day become only the gently alternating moments of a "perpetual communion."

In Teilhard's *Notes de Rétraites*, he often expressed difficulty with the prayer of St. Ignatius. But Teilhard never seemed to consider the Ignatian Examen. St. Ignatius would take the events of the day just finished and see how we have lived them, making them his prayer. Teilhard has us take the events of the day about to begin and dedicate them before we live them; this makes each event a communion with Jesus. Both St. Ignatius and Teilhard would agree that the events of our lives constitute the material of such prayer: St. Ignatius as the day ends and Teilhard as the day begins.

BIBLIOGRAPHY

Abbreviations for Works by Teilhard de Chardin

A *Activation of Energy*, translated by Rene Hague. New York: Harcourt Brace Jovanovich, 1963.

C *Christianity & Evolution*, translated by Rene Hague. New York: Harcourt Brace, 1971.

Cor Correspondence: Pierre Teilhard de Chardin and Maurice Blondel, edited and annotated by Henri de Lubac. New York: Herder & Herder, 1967.

D *The Divine Milieu*, translator unidentified. New York: Harper & Row; first Harper Torchbook edition, 1965.

F *The Future of Man*, translated by Norman Denny. New York: Harper Colophon, 1964.

HE *Human Energy*, translated by J. M. Cohen. New York: Harcourt Brace Jovanovich, 1969.

HM *The Heart of Matter*, translated by Rene Hague. New York: Harcourt Brace Jovanovich, 1978.

HU *Hymn of the Universe*, translated by Simon Bartholomew. London: Collins, 1965.

J *Journal, Tome I, 26 aout, 1915–4 janvier, 1919, texte intégral publié par Nicole et Karl Schmitz-Moorman*. Paris: Fayard, 1975.

J, followed by a date. Unpublished journals of Teilhard. Copies of these may be viewed in the Georgetown University Archives.

LE *Letters from Egypt, 1905–1908*, introduced and annotated by Henri de Lubac, translated by Mary Ilford. New York: Herder & Herder, 1965.

LGI *Lettres de Guerre Inedite*, par Teilhard et Jean Boussac, presentee par François Guillaumont. Paris: O.E.I.L., c. 1986.

LH *Letters from Hastings*, introduced and edited by Henri de Lubac, translated by Judith de Stefano. New York: Herder & Herder, 1968.

Li *Lettres intimes à Auguste Valensin, Bruno de Solages, et Henri de Lubac, introduction et notes par Henri de Lubac*. Paris: Editions Aubier-Montaigne, 1972.

LJM *Lettres à Jeanne Mortier*. Paris: Editions de Seuil, 1984.

169

LLZ   *Letters to Leontine Zanta*, translated by Bernard Wall, introductions by Robert Garric and Henri de Lubac. New York: Harper & Row, 1968.

LMF   *Letters from My Friend Teilhard de Chardin*, translated by Mary Lukas. New York: Paulist Press, 1979.

LP   *Letters from Paris, 1912–1914*, introduced and annotated by Henri de Lubac, translated by Michael Mazzarese. New York: Herder & Herder, 1967.

LS   *Letters of Teilhard de Chardin and Lucile Swan*, edited by Thomas M. King, S.J. and Mary Wood Gilbert, introduction by Pierre Leroy, S.J. Scranton: Scranton University Press, 2002; originally Georgetown University Press, 1993.

LT   *Letters from a Traveler*, translated by Bernard Wall. New York and Evanston: Harper & Row, 1962.

LTF   *Letters to Two Friends*. New York and Cleveland: World Publishing, 1969.

MM   *The Making of a Mind*, translated by Rene Hague. New York: Harper & Row, 1965.

Nr   *Notes de retraites: 1919–1954, introduction et notes de Gerard-Henry Baudry, Preface de Gustave Martelet, S.J.* Paris: Seuil, 2003.

Os   *L'Oeuvre scientifique, 10 tomes, textes réunis et édités par Nicole & Karl Schmitz-Moormann, preface de Jean Piveteau.* Olten and Freiburg im Breisgau: Walter-Verlag, 1971.

P   *The Phenomenon of Man*, translated by Bernard Wall. New York: Harper & Row, 1969.

S   *Science & Christ*, translated by Rene Hague. New York: Harper & Row, 1968.

T   *Towards the Future*, translated by Rene Hague. New York: Harcourt Brace Jovanovich, 1975.

TenC   *Teilhard de Chardin en Chine, correspondence inédité [1923– 1940].* The letters of Teilhard to Marcellin Boule with commentary and annotations by Amelie Vialet and Arnaud Hurel of the Museum of Natural History. Paris: Editions Edisud, 2004.

UL   Unpublished letter, followed by initials or name of addressee and date. Copies of these may be seen in the Georgetown University Archives.

V   *The Vision of the Past*, translated by J. M. Cohen. New York: Harper & Row, 1966.

W   *Writings in Time of War*, translated by Rene Hague. New York: Harper & Row, 1968.

Abbreviations of Works by Other Authors

Andersson   *Children of the Yellow Earth: Studies in Prehistoric China*, by J. Gunnar Andersson, translated by E. Classen. London: Keegan Paul, Trench, Trubner, 1934; paperback edition by MIT Press, 1973.

Barbour   *In the Field with Teilhard de Chardin*, by George Barbour. New York: Herder and Herder, 1965.

Corte   *Pierre Teilhard de Chardin, His Life and Spirit*, by Nicolas Corte, translated by Martin Jarrett-Kerr. New York: Macmillan, 1960.

CU   *The Cloud of Unknowing and Other Writings*, author unknown; translated into contemporary English by Clifton Wolton. London: Penguin, 1961.

Cuenot   *Teilhard de Chardin, a Biographical Study*, by Claude Cuenot, translated by Vincent Colimore. London: Burns & Oates, 1965.

De Lubac RT   *The Religion of Teilhard de Chardin*, by Henri de Lubac, S.J., translated by Rene Hague. Garden City: Doubleday, 1968.

De Lubac TMM   *Teilhard de Chardin: The Man and his Meaning*, by Henri de Lubac, S.J., translated by Rene Hague. New York: New American Library, 1965

De Terra   *Memories of Teilhard de Chardin*, by Helmut De Terra, translated from the German by J. Maxwell Brownjohn. London: Collins, 1964.

Dos   *The Brothers Karamazov*, by Fyodor Dostoyevsky, translated by Constance Garnett. New York: The Modern Library, 1930.

GM   *Gift and Mystery: On the Fiftieth Anniversary of My Priesthood*, by Pope John Paul II. New York: Doubleday, 1996.

Jia   *The Story of Peking Man*, by Jia Lanpo and Huang Weiwen. London and New York: Oxford University Press, 1990.

King   *Teilhard's Mysticism of Knowing*, by Thomas M. King, S.J. New York: Seabury, 1981.

Kropf   *Teilhard, Scripture, and Revelation*, by Richard W. Kropf. Rutherford: Farleigh Dickenson University Press, c. 1980.

Lukas   *Teilhard*, by Mary and Ellen Lukas. New York: McGraw Hill, 1981; originally published by Doubleday, 1977.

Merton   *The Seven Storey Mountain*, by Thomas Merton. New York: Harcourt Brace Jovanovich, First Harvest Edition, 1999; originally published, 1948.

Nemeck   *Teilhard de Chardin et Jean de la Croix*, by Francis Kelly Nemeck. Montreal: Bellarmin, 1975.

Or   *Origins*, May 1, 2003. Vol. 32, No. 46, #8.

Pieper   *Leisure the Basis of Culture*, by Josef Pieper, new translation by Gerald Malsbury, introduction by Roger Scruton. South Bend: St. Augustine's Press, 1998.

Ratzinger   *The Spirit of the Liturgy*, by Joseph Cardinal Ratzinger, translated by John Saward. San Francisco: Ignatius Press, 2000.

Ringgren   *The Messiah in the Old Testament*, by Helmet Ringgren. London: SCM Press, 1956.

Speight   *Teilhard de Chardin: A Biography*, by Robert Speight. London: William Clowes & Sons, 1967.

Swisher   *Java Man*, by Carl C. Swisher, Garniss H. Curtis, and Roger Lewin. New York: Scribner, 2000.

TUK   *Teilhard and the Unity of Knowledge*, edited by Thomas M. King, S.J., and James F. Salmon, S.J. Ramsey: Paulist Press, 1983.